The Warrior's Guide To Insanity

Traumatic Stress and Life

- For My Brothers and Sisters -

By

Sgt. PTSD Brandi

U.S.M.C. Never Retired?

www.sgtbrandi.com

*This book is dedicated to my
Brother and Sister Warriors
as well as their Families,
Loved Ones and Friends.*

*To all those now suffering
the aftermath of war,
I say to each of you,
live by Courage,
the strength of a Warrior
and hold fast to the
Sacred Code of Honor.*

Table of Contents

Introduction

In this brutally open and honest book, I am allowing each of you to pass over a long-guarded threshold. This secret world is the inner sanctum of a Warrior: a hidden place, seldom spoken of to the uninitiated, yet a time honored world in which we live every moment of every year. My reasons for releasing this work are clear. We are now at war again, and all Warriors share the same battleground, being caught between two very different and conflicting worlds.

Each of us left behind the comforts and safety of our country to experience the horrors of war, and yet within it, we found the true meaning of Trust, Honor, Friendship and Loss. As our tours ended, we returned stateside only to find our torment continuing with the painful memories of how life once was, and yet could never be again. Due to my own military background, I have kept the primary focus of this "Warriors Guide" aimed directly at our armed forces, yet anyone having developed Post Traumatic Stress will quickly realize how much we all have in common, both civilian and military alike.

This work recounts many of my own experiences, beginning as a Marine combat rifleman, with Hotel Company, 2nd Battalion, 7th Marines in and around Chu Lai, South Vietnam. However, it is not "my" story, but the vivid reality of many thousands like myself, who learned first to survive combat, and for nearly 40 years, have learned to survive life. Where necessary, I use harsh language. Some examples and stories may be harsh as well. However, I venture to say that if you were a timid soul, you wouldn't be holding this book.

Be advised, I'm cutting you some slack in the first section, gotta' ease you into the book a bit. Sort a like your first 5 mile forced march with full gear, when every muscle of your out-of-shape body aches and you feel like droppin' out. But like my Old Sarge used to say, "Pain is Good! Now feel the Goodness!" Not to worry, because after a while you'll be "lean, mean, fighting machines," kickin' ass on your traumatic experiences (no name taking allowed). I know that many of you still feel like you're on patrol, cut off, and behind enemy lines. But don't sweat it! The choppers are on the way! And this time, everybody gets out!

Now, in true Marine Corps fashion, "Lock and Load!" and "Listen Up!" Your life is on the line.

Prologue

To Family and Friends

For those of you who love your Warrior, your Son, Daughter, Husband, Wife and Friend, I'm offering you a chance to understand Why they've come home from war forever changed, forged in battle and now home with you once again. Imagine going to work each morning and never knowing if you were going to die that day, or perhaps at best, be severely wounded. This is in fact what your loved one feels; it's how they live every single day of combat in Afghanistan and Iraq.

Because they can't talk to you about their experiences, because they feel nervous in crowds, sit with their back to the wall in restaurants, don't like parties, check for snipers on the roof of Wal-Mart, or can't drive their cars for fear of an ambush, doesn't mean they don't love you. It only means they are struggling to survive in a world that's now become as alien as the surface of the moon.

Warriors truly want to feel normal, they want to be like they were and what you would like them to be again, but that is impossible; they have changed forever. Help them to help themselves by understanding what they have been through, what horrors they have experienced and how they long only to be loved and accepted for who they've now become.

For a Warrior walking off the battlefield, the journey of life becomes very lonely, very painful. All of us ask only for someone to care, to understand our pain and to love us as Warriors who gave all we had to protect what we hold sacred, our country, our home and our loved ones.

The "Warrior's Guide to Insanity" may help you to know just a little of how we feel, how we pray for a life in a world so precious to us and yet lies just beyond our grasp. A little part of all of us dies when we experience war. But what is left is all we have and with that small hope, we cling to life; the hope of being accepted, the hope of perhaps one day being loved, to feel a little joy in our lives and at long last to feel some small measure of peace.

Continue on if you will, and as you read this work, ask

yourself, "How can I help the one I love? How can I unconditionally love them and help them to feel purpose in their life once again?"

Warriors love those they leave behind, more than they will ever know. I ask you now, to open your hearts to us, to allow us to be a part of your world that we would willingly die to protect. We will never be like we were before war. Accept us for who we have now become, for what we have sacrificed for you and this great Nation.

Most Respectfully,

Sgt. Brandi, United States Marine Corps

Acknowledgments

It is important to thank all of the many Veterans I have known over the long and difficult years since the Vietnam Era. Each of these Warriors has had their own story to tell, of their lives, their struggles and their triumphs. And each of these brave Souls has served this Nation without question, placing their lives on the line for the principles they held sacred.

Many are now my own personal memories, of cherished Friends and fallen Heroes. And if I had not crossed paths with these honorable men and women along my own journey, it would not have been possible to write this work for our Young Warriors of today. I thank you all, my Brothers and Sisters, both from the past and the present.

I thank you for your Sacrifices and Service, your Honor and Courage. You are what I believe to be the finest example of the Nobility of the Human Spirit, and I am proud to be a Warrior by your side.

I would also like to thank my dear "Friends" for their support as well: Karin Brandi for your honesty and wisdom; Margaret Wolverton for your encouragement and superb editing skills; Jane Chanik also for your encouragement and computer skills (I was hopelessly lost). And finally, to a good Friend and fellow Warrior, who would prefer his name not be mentioned.

You are all very wise and compassionate individuals, deeply concerned, as am I, about our Young Veterans in Afghanistan, Iraq, and now returning stateside. It is a privilege and Honor that I may call each of you "Friend".

On behalf of the many thousands of men and women in the Armed Services of this nation, I also wish to thank Jennifer, Dan, Amanda and the highly skilled and professional staff of Roller Printing for their concerned guidance and assistance in printing this work. Also Margaret at Mad Margaret Publishing, Inc. located at madmargaretpublishing@earthlink.net, for her tireless effort and assistance in the preparation of this book. These two companies have been instrumental in getting this Warrior's Guide into circulation as quickly and inexpensively as is possible for a self-published book. "The Warrior's Guide to Insanity" is now available to all who need it, in print, podcast and CD.

Section One: War is Our Business and Business is Good

1-1 The Death of Innocence

The tragedies of war are timeless. Killing is the same now in the deserts of Afghanistan and Iraq as it was in the jungles of Vietnam, or in any other war for that matter. Every warrior who has walked out onto the battlefield has shared the same feelings in common. We all controlled our fear, we all moved forward to engage the enemy, as adrenaline pumped through every fiber of our body. We killed before being killed, and when it was all over, we trembled from exhaustion, thanked God to be alive, and moved out to the next battle. This continues until you're either dead, severely wounded, or finish your tour and are sent home.

When you kill another human being for the first time, something changes inside of you. Doesn't matter what emotions are going on inside your head during the killing, such as hate, anger, fear, or revenge. These feelings only delay the results a bit, because eventually, what you **just did** comes back around to bite you right on the ass. I'll give you an example.

Intelligence reports had just come in from headquarters that a large shipment of arms and supplies were being sent down the river near our base camp. This meant that the Viet Cong in our area would have a fresh supply of guns and ammo to bring us a nice little house warming gift about 03:00 in the morning. Those of less than great wisdom decided the answer to this problem was to set up an ambush on "our" river and capture all the goodies. Well, being a gung-ho Marine, and well trained (for a whole week!) in guerilla tactics back in the land of fruits and nuts (California), I naturally volunteered to kill a "Commie for Christ." This was my first night ambush, and I was ready long before it got dark.

Everything takes on a veil of gray and black when the sun sets. It also gets a little spooky when you think that one of those shadows might in fact be one of the Little People waiting to blow your young ass back to America. At night you walk differently, you listen more carefully, and you stay as quiet as possible. When at last the order came to "saddle up!", everyone grabbed a few extra grenades, a couple extra magazines of ammo, and headed out. I had already painted my face with black grease stick, so I thought I was ahead of the program. Man, was I in for a surprise.

I started to feel a little nervous as we cleared the last check point and moved onto the trail leading to the river. The moon was out, but I thought "Shit, how the hell do you see anything out here?" Being a dumb ass, and new to the Nam, I just followed along, figurin' the point man knew the way. What seemed like hours was actually only about 20 minutes, when we finally reached the river. The corporal in charge was very organized, and told me to take the first position up stream, which meant I would trigger the ambush. Feeling pleased with myself about being in the lead position, I eagerly made my way up near the river's edge and started to wait.

As amazing as it sounds, when you're exhausted it's next to impossible to stay awake, life threatening situation or not. Even at 18 years old and in good shape, after filling sand bags for most of the day, and pulling watch the night before, I was pretty well wiped out. About two hours had passed, and I still couldn't see very far out over the river, but suddenly, I could hear the swish of a paddle coming my way. I came to full alert, and my heart was pounding so loud I thought everyone could hear it. As I was trying to control my breathing, thoughts were runnin' through my brain: "Damn, I wonder if all those other guys are asleep?" and remembering my night-firing exercises back at Camp Pendleton, "You can't miss, even in the dark!"

At last I could barely make out two boats floating past my position, about 30 feet from shore. "I had to let them move into the kill zone," I thought, slowly moving my trigger finger forward. As I picked my target, the safety "clicked" off, and I opened fire!

Instantly, the entire line opened up, and the deafening roar of an M-60 machine gun and a fire team with M-14's, every fifth round a tracer, was very impressive. In not more than 45 seconds the corporal gave the order to cease fire! All was dead still, except for the ringing in my ears. There were no signs of movement coming from the boats. Immediately, several Marines waded out into the shallow, muddy water and began pulling the bodies to shore. One by one, out they came, and bit by agonizing bit my heart was ripped out of my chest, by the irreversible finality of what I had just done.

All I could say was "Oh my God NO!" "Please God NO!" "Not Children!"

Except for one wrinkled up old man, we had killed 14 children that night. And it was all I could do to keep from screaming out loud. Turned inward, that screaming still goes on. Out of anger, one Marine broke, yelling "You fucking bastard!", as he pumped five more rounds into the old man's body. I just stood there motionless for a time, staring at those little bodies, asking God to "make this not be true."

Leaning on my rifle and slowly kneeling to the bank of the river, I reached out to gently touch the cold, lifeless face of one especially beautiful little girl. And in one undeniable, horrifying moment, as my hand touched her cheek, I felt as though everything inside of me had collapsed. A numbness fell over me. Who I was had died with those children.

What changed in me after that first killing was that I could no longer feel anything close to the joys or innocence of youth. I became more quiet, more withdrawn, and in some ways less satisfied with my duties as a warrior. At that time, I couldn't get over the stillness of the human body when it was dead, and that "I" had caused it. Killing adult soldiers was one thing, but killing my first kid just about ripped my guts out.

The whole situation was very confusing, because I was a warrior, trained to kill, and doing a damn good job of it. So why was I feeling anything at all? I don't know if it was fortunate or unfortunate, but by the time I left Vietnam, I had done so much killing, that I didn't feel much of anything anymore. At least that's what I thought.

Our young combat troops now returning home know exactly what I'm saying. You've probably killed adults, and probably killed kids. You feel numb inside and don't really give a shit about very much. You've lost some of the best friends you've ever had, and you'd like to just forget about the whole damn thing for awhile, maybe for good. Well my friends, "It don't work that way."

4

Many times, I tried stayin' drunk for a few days at a time. You know, "just for the hell of it" I told myself. But what I was really trying to do was to find some peace, a kind of escape for a little while. Veterans back in the 60's were pretty much on their own to figure things out. We also had to maintain a very low profile, because a lot of folks looked at us as "baby killing monsters."

Here is one point I want to make right away for our new war Veterans, and to the people of this country. No one I have ever known felt good about killing! However, like it or not, it **is** part of any war, so you civilians need to deal with it. There is no good way to kill a human being.

And yeah, children do get caught up in the battles and the killing as well. Sometimes they're even the ones trying to kill you! So what is a Warrior suppose to do? Just say, "Oh, it's OK honey, come right over here, sit on my lap and pull the pin. We'll just have a big huggie, while you blow our asses off the face of the earth?" Don't think so.

It's real easy to judge someone when you're looking in from the outside of a situation. And I sure as hell hope that over the past thirty-plus years, Americans have learned not to judge so quickly, and this time, cut our Young Warriors some slack.

Well anyway, there's an old saying that "No matter where you go, there you are." And each time I'd sober up, no shit, there I was still lookin' at the faces of everyone I'd wasted, and being haunted by the dead brothers I'd lost. There was no getting away from the uncomfortable memories during the day, and the nightmares whenever I could fall asleep. This is happening "Right Now" with many of our Young Veterans.

PTSD (Post Traumatic Stress Disorder) wasn't a catchy little phrase back in the 60's. In those days the shrinkers called the effects of combat Battle Fatigue or Shell Shock. Doesn't matter what anyone calls it, the fact is, it really sucks when you've got it.

Remember I said I was gonna go easy on you for a bit? Well, here's the good news first! You Youngins don't have to duplicate what I did. That means, you don't have to wade through all the shit by yourself, because now you have a lot of support, and not just from us Old Knuckle Draggers either (but rest assured, we've still got your 6 O'clock). And, (more good news) because of all the help these days, you won't be blind-sided by emotions that you have no idea how to deal with. That really makes a big difference.

Now for the bad news. Be advised, you **will** be feeling the **same** things I did. Every Warrior has. But we're gonna' go though each one of these issues, and you'll know exactly how to deal with'em and how to be an "A. J. Squared Away" in your deep-fried brain.

So then, let's just focus on the possibility that you've killed a bunch of people, maybe even capped a bunch of kids, called in a few air strikes or artillery on houses filled with civilians, and now you feel confused, depressed, and maybe angry. And you just can't get your brain-housing-group to make any sense out of all the feelings and emotions.

Well guess what? There's nothing **WRONG** with your feelings! That's right! You **are** a human being, and humans are suppose to **FEEL**. Don't worry, if you're still a little numb like I was, it'll all come out eventually, and you'll deal with it when it does. And once again, be advised, one day it definitely **will** be right in your face, up close and personal. We'll talk later about how to kick ass on that topic too.

So look, cut yourself some slack right now. Because one thing is for sure. You can't kill people and not be screwed up. You can't watch your friends get blown up in front of you and not have nightmares for a time. I've been there, seen it, felt it, and I'm still sittin' here talkin' to "you".

So don't feel like the Lone Ranger on this one, because you're not. I know a lot of Combat Vets, and every single one of them has gone down exactly the same road as you. We have all had to make the choice, to either go on and see what life has in store for us, or give up and drop out pukin', maybe even do something stupid like commit suicide. We'll talk about that later too.

No bullshit, you're gonna be in a world of hurt for a time, but there **are** ways to make it out of the bush a little quicker and a little easier. No need to low crawl through half your life, when with the right tactics, you can reach your objective quickly. We'll cover all that as we move along here. Just don't wimp out. Keep reading even if it hurts, and it most likely will.

Also keep in mind, that anyone who has experienced war, and anyone who has faced death has had a life changing experience. I don't care if it's a near fatal car accident, a gang-banger firefight, a building engulfed in flames that collapses just as you walk out, a mutilated kid that you can't resuscitate who dies in your arms, watching the Twin Towers collapse with your loved ones inside, or pickin' up body parts after it did. You ain't gonna' be the same person when it's over.

"What do I do now?" you ask. You grit your teeth, and read on! You let this old Jar Head walk you down your own personal trail of tears, and get a grip on how to make it to the next extraction point, to a new life. It may not be the life you now have, but it **can** be a life that one day will bring a little peace in your days, maybe even a little joy back in planning your tomorrows.

Now, let's get on with it! And don't worry, I'm runnin' point for you on this one. I've cleared the path ahead. So jam a full magazine in your rifle! **Safeties Off!** We're movin' out!!

I don't want to dwell on this too much, but let's get real. These first few lines here are mostly for the Moms and Dads out there, so Listen Up! Unless you've been a Warrior in combat, you ain't gonna understand squat shit from watchin' "Mash," "Rambo," or documentaries on PBS. You sure as hell aren't gonna' get anything out the ambulance chasin' nightly news.

Hey Mom and Dad, are you payin' attention?

What you might consider is that your son or daughter just got back from a war. That's right, a real "War" where they had to do things and see things that you can't imagine. When they either come back on leave, or are back for good, you've got to get rid of the idea that, "Oh, my sweet little boy or girl is a good little boy or girl, they wouldn't do anything like that."

Save them a little frustration from your own denial. And face it, they are not the same little podunk-eaten, candy-ass kids they were while growin' up. They returned as adults, and full blown Warriors! You can't possibly understand what they've been through, any more than you can understand what people went through watching the Towers go down, unless you had someone you loved in them like they did. The point is, Mom and Dad, if you haven't shared the same exact experiences as your kids, then you're not gonna know **how** they feel. That's just the way it works.

Now for you Vets, returning to the land of the Big PX (Post Exchange), your parents can give you a big sloppy kiss, cry, hug you, and repeat a hundred times how much they "missed their baby," then chew your ass out for putting them through all the worry. Or, they may not want to talk at all about your experiences, like mine. Who knows what they're gonna say or do, and who really gives a shit?

Sometimes parents and/or the whole family, will go through the one day "Welcome back" routine, and then expect you to be just like you were, and not have a clue why you're not. I've swapped a lot of stories like this with other Vets over the years, so you're not the only one who's gonna go through this or something similar. Maybe you already have?

After I had about all the welcome home I could stand, I slipped out and thought maybe I could nab a beer or two with my fake ID card down at the local VFW (Veterans of Foreign Wars).

I first need to say is that the VFW in the 60's was NOT what it is today. And that today it's a fine group of Old Warriors, mostly from the Vietnam period, with a few left from Korea. Back then, it was something else.

Showing my military ID and walking up to the bar, I sat down and ordered a cool one. The bar tender raised an eyebrow, but gave me the beer anyway. Mind you, I was only a young pup, just 19 years old.

Taking a hearty swig, and looking around, for a moment I thought I'd mistakenly wandered in to the geriatric clinic at the V.A. (Veterans Administration). But the beer was cold, and I sure as hell needed the alcohol.

On the second round, a couple of old guys came over and sat down next to me. That was OK, but I really just wanted to be alone and concentrate on the "golden nectar" in front of me. And that's when it started.

One old timer asked me what branch I was in? I could have been a smart ass and said the one in the tree out back, but I respectfully replied, the Marine Corps. Then he made his first big mistake by saying, "Yeah, some of my best friends are Marines." You know how **that** feels if you are from an ethnic minority. It's like when I grew up an Italian, and everyone felt the need to tell me all of their retarded Italian jokes first, then assure me that "some of their best friends were wops." Never seemed that funny to me, coming from a bigot.

Well anyway, the old Vet looked drunk, and I was trying to get there, so I let it slide. Sucking down the second beer in record speed, I ordered another, thinking maybe this jerk-off will go away soon. He didn't, and my patience was growing thin.

Then he asked if I had been to Vietnam. I replied, that I was on leave and had just served in a combat line company, and that I'd really rather not talk about it. As he went on to tell me how Vietnam "wasn't a real war," and maybe I

9

should have a drink somewhere else, I began to think, "where is somewhere else?"

He was too old to punch his lights out, so I chugged my last beer at the VFW, and walked out considering a return visit with a nice, heart-warming-thank-you-gift for each of them. That would have been a small box with a red bow on top and a card that read:

"Pull the little pin on the side, and count to seven."

So why am I talking about all this? It's because the VFW is now a real fine place to go and be around Warriors that are not gonna judge you. There are also a number of other support organizations as well, and I guarantee, you'll be treated with respect. Most likely, there will soon be (if there aren't already) organizations tailored just for Veterans from Afghanistan and Iraq. At least check out a few of these. Your local Veterans Outreach Center will have a list. We're gonna talk a lot more about support later, but for now, keep a few things in your head.

Going from video games to actual war is quite a transition, and once again (for my fellow Marines) you are feeling exactly what you're supposed to feel. So if you have more control than I did, but still need to get away from the source of irritation (family?) as swiftly as possible, do so **without guilt**. If you need a "Brain Break," maybe you can find someone from your unit, another combat Vet or a real friend with similar experiences to sort things out a bit. If you can't find anyone for the moment, it's better to be alone in a quiet place than it is to be around people that don't understand, and/or irritate the hell out of you.

I used to like the Military Cemetery. It was quiet, I could be among friends, and nobody bothered me. Being a little smarter now(?), I think hangin' out with some buddies at the VFW, or from your old unit would be a better choice. I was pretty desperate in those days, and you sure as hell don't have to be.

Hang on to those thoughts, while you're joggin' in place. I've gotta keep you in shape for the next topic!

Remember, **NO** quitters allowed, so put a piece of leather in your teeth and keep readin' on.

You may ask "Will I ever be the same?" My answer is simple. Hell NO! So you may as well get that in your head right now, deal with it, and start working on the **New You**. Having killed, or having been witness to it, having been in any life threatening event where you walked away and others didn't, has changed your life for the rest of your life. You will never be the same person that you were before that experience.

Think about it. What were you like before the war or other life threatening experience? What things did you like? What made you happy? Where did you like to go? What kind of music or movies did you enjoy? Did you like a lot of friends around? And the list goes on. I'm gonna guess that most of that stuff is ancient history now, and that's all right, so are You!

I really wish some old dumb ass Marine would have said to me, "Boy! **There's nothin' wrong with who you are, you just ain't who you use to be!** Now drop down and give me 50, while you think about it!"

So what does this mean? It means you now have to find out "Who" you are, "What" you like, and who you want to be around. It really isn't that hard to think about, if you're honest with yourself. But that may be difficult to do, if you're living your life the way other people want you to live. Chances are, if this **is** the case, you're miserable anyway, so why not make a few changes?

The long haired, brain-fried, acid freaks in the 60's would have said "Man, this is a righteous gig." That means, it is a great chance to do whatever you want. Some Vets I knew went off the save the world and finally figured out they had to save themselves first. Some went off with a crystal hung around their necks humming through the woods until they found some poor unsuspecting tree to hug. Others joined biker gangs (I mean "clubs"), preferring a taste of outlaw company. Some changed jobs, or went back to school for a new career. Many dropped out of society completely. And a few even changed their names. The point is, you can do whatever you want, and you can decide, just for you alone, what's gonna bring a little joy into your life.

Unfortunately, many of the old Vets like me, learned the hard way. Over the years, we slowly and painfully tried to **pretend** we were the same as we always were, the same as everyone else, while dragging our families and dip-shit friends through our rage and nightmares. There were a few exceptions however, and a few Combat Vets did finally manage to get along with female companions of like mind; crazy people like crazy people? But, I was the usual slow learner in that battlefield, and it wasn't until my third wife divorced me that I finally figured out that maybe I'm better off being single.

You see, no matter where you end up, as long as the choice is yours, and you're making your own honest decisions, it's OK! You're gonna fit in somewhere, so just decide where. Hell, I'm not center-of-bubble at times, but when I stopped pretending, my life worked out great. Better than B Street in Okinawa on payday (you'll have to ask a Vet about that one, or check the glossary).

If you haven't got the message yet, you may be lookin' at a whole new life. That may mean friends, jobs and locations, the whole enchilada. Believe me, it's a lot better to find out who you are right now and start your "new" life, than it is to experiment for nearly 40 years. I've had over 60 jobs, 4 major career changes, three wives, lived all over the country, and it took 6 colleges and 20 years to get a degree I never use (toilet paper?). It sometimes takes Marines a little longer I guess, at least this one.

Now, part of the reason I had so many jobs was because a gear slipped loose in my Brain Housing Group, and there wasn't anybody around to identify it and send out for replacement parts. You're not livin' in that same empty, un-staffed supply depot.

You may find it a tad unusual that I've had so many jobs. But this is actually the norm and not the exception for many Vets from my era. I think the record in fact was held by another Recon Marine, who got "left" in North Vietnam when the politicians finally pulled the handle on the big green toilet. He had to fight his way through Laos, and then to Thailand, to find friendlies and get back to the States.

We were both in Phoenix, Arizona at the time, and attending a weekly meeting for Combat Vets. After the "gathering" was over and everyone had slipped back into the shadows, this other Jar Head and I were laughing about something, when he asked me, "How many jobs you had since gettin' out of the Crotch?" (The Crotch is what **only** Marines may reverently call the Marine Corps).

Since you can say anything to another combat Vet, I wasn't the least embarrassed to admit that my count at that time was about 38. He looked at me and started to laugh again. Then he said, " I've had 47 jobs in 46 days!" We stayed there for about another hour laughing and talking about all the dick heads we'd worked for, then we too slipped into the night, pretending to be normal like all the other civvies.

Take a lesson from this. Do you want a track record like I have, or do you want to be smarter, and get your act together now? No sweat, if you've got 40 or 50 years to kill. But I would have been a hell of a lot happier for a hell of a lot longer if I'd have started a long time ago. So don't be discouraged, and don't give up; no quitters allowed on my duty watch. I'm here to tell ya, that after all the bullshit in my life, I know who I am, what I am, and I'm truly happy since I don't pretend for other people. And if I can do it, **"So Can YOU!"** And you will.

What I'm saying is this. No matter how bad you feel right now, you CAN feel better later. No matter what guilt you're dumpin' on yourself, with a little time and work, you can sort out the shit, and get onto what makes you feel good about yourself. And I don't give a rat's ass if you're depressed! There is nothing wrong with your reactions, or you. Although the legal drug cartel would like you to think so, you are **not** gonna be on the zombie meds your whole life either. Hell, maybe not at all.

Oh, and by the way, the counselor at the Veterans Outreach Center isn't gonna be hiding a syringe of mood stabilizers to stab in your neck as you walk through the door. If you don't want the drugs, "Just Say No". That simple.

All you really need to do to start feeling better is to start feeling better about **you**, admit you could use a little help, learn how to deal with the problems, and start planning your new life. I guarantee, that once you've decided what you truly want to do, where you want to go, and how you want your life to unfold, it'll be like a kid looking forward to a trip to Disneyland.

But don't start settin' the "live-trap" for Mickey Mouse just yet, you'll need to keep reading, to figure out which path your gonna take to the Magic Kingdom. There's the long, hard way, and there's the shorter hard way. Both paths lead uphill, but it's worth the climb. So then, in the words of my own wise and knowing Sarge,

"Keep your chin up, your head down, and one round in the chamber, in case you stick the bayonet!"

Remember, we're cuttin' you some slack in the first few topics. Lettin' you ease into things a bit.

But stay alert!   Now, let's "Move Out!

1-4 What is Reality?

Reality for you is **not** the same as it is for everyone else. What I'm trying to say here is that you now have a very clear understanding of the difference of what is real and the bullshit illusion that most people live in. Well now, that seems about as clear as mud. I'd better give you some examples.

Let's suppose you've just returned stateside from a delightful brain-frying vacation in the Ocean of Fire. You've nabbed a couple of your favorite barf-in-the-bag burgers from the local grease pit on your way home, and you've just settled down with chow and a couple of cool ones in front of the boob-tube. "A-ah," you think, " just like old times."

You've heard about the new "Reality" programs on some of the TV networks, and your now twitchy brain is interested and wants to check'em out. While bolting down your food like a monitor lizard (you've learned to eat fast while on vacation) and scanning through the channels you're thinking "What the fuck, over! (Marine saying)," and "What the hell is this bullshit!" It may be entertainment for some people to watch a bunch of podunk-eaters, carrying pretty backpacks to bum-fuck Egypt, some crybaby non-hackers, livin' on an island, bitchin' about each other, or a bunch of dip-shits locked up in a psycho ward in L.A., but this ain't reality! It sure as hell ain't reality to you anymore. Maybe it never was.

Even though your brain may feel like a sweat bee drowning in your soup on a hot day, like it or not, your reality **is** clear and very different. You now know that a bullet, traveling at 2000+ feet per second can end your life, taking away every dream you've ever had in the past, and every plan you'll ever have for the future. You now understand how the Angel of Death is ever present, awaiting Her call at every minute, and you've learned to enjoy every minute just in case. "One Day at a Time" has become your reality. You are now living in the present moment! Hey, that's not so bad, it "just sucks" the way you had to get there.

Look at it this way: a lot of people walk around with their head up their ass, worrying about the past that they sure as hell can't change, or the future that hasn't even come yet.

They skip right over the present, which in my simple way of lookin' at things, is the only damn reality we've got.

What do I mean by "reality," you ask? Well, once again, I like to keep things simple. Reality to me just means something that is "real", actual, and/or "true". You know, something that actually exists. Touchie-feelie sort of stuff. By the way, this Old Knuckle Dragger also believes that "thoughts" are very real things; been around the block to many times not to. We'll talk about thoughts at the end of this book, but be advised: thoughts can be very helpful, or as destructive as a .308 round entering center of mass. It's no bullshit about wishing either.

Ever heard that saying, "Be careful what you wish for"? That's one, you definitely do not want'a mess around with. Here's a couple more! Never, ever say, "What else can go wrong?" Or "Can things get any worse?" because Murphy, the fates, the universe, or whatever you want'a call it, seems to be hangin' around like a crow on a picket fence, waiting for your young ass to slip up and utter one of those sayings. Then sure as shit, things do go wrong, and the situation does get worse. I hate to think how many times I've tried this one out, and it never failed.

Hey! Are you feeling a little like "Things are gonna be OK" inside yet? Don't worry, you will. Let's keep movin' out on this topic.

Alright, so now besides knowing how fine a line we walk with Death, and living in the moment, you've also learned, or you are about to learn to live by a new perspective.

It goes like this: "Don't sweat the little things, and if it's NOT life threatening, it sure as hell "is" a little thing." This attitude is very healthy, because it leads to a very helpful way of thinking.

I call this new way of thinking, the **"I don't give a shit attitude"**. Let's see how it works. Suppose my so called "friends" think I'm a wacko, and don't like me anymore (which they did). I say, "I don't give a shit!" "I'll find other crazy people just like me (which I did)." Let's say my

17

girlfriend just dumped me because I now sleep with a loaded .45 pistol that I love more than her. I say, "I don't give a shit." I've still got my pistol. You see, it takes the pressure off. So what I'm trying to point out here, is that you look at life a whole lot differently now, and that's "Good!" You just have to learn how to adapt to it in any way that works for you.

Oh, and by the way, if you haven't figured it out yet, "shit" is at the very foundation of a Marine's vocabulary; once mastered, this highly useful word can be used as every part of speech, adding zest and color in describing any situation. Use your imagination in deciding what the other most often used, four letter word is? This one also takes great focus and concentration. My Old Sarge, was truly a Great Sentence Master of these two treasured words. At his prime, he was able to use both of these time honored words in the same sentence, replacing all other parts of speech. A fine example of true Marine Discipline!

Now remember, I said to cut yourself some slack? You're just gonna have to ride out a few waves once and a while. And of course, it hurts your feelings when the people who were suppose to love you unconditionally are now on the phone calling Animal Control. My first impulse in those situations (and there were some ugly ones) was, "when in doubt, empty the magazine."

This was definitely **NOT** a good way to think. More than once, I just about ended up at the Federal Hyatt Regency, with Bubba and his endless supply of Vaseline as a house guest. Not the way to go. It's much better just to say "I don't give a shit," because it ain't life threatening. You'll also have to understand that it wasn't because they really weren't worth the 15 cents a round (for a .308). They just weren't worth goin' to jail over. Never met anyone that was.

Remember, there is nothing wrong with feeling emotions. It's how you're suppose to react to stressful situations; sometimes that keeps us alive. You just can't act out in the way you'd like to at times. My VA counselor once told me, "You can kill everyone you want in your mind, just don't do it in the street," and "the more you keep working on feeling better about yourself, the sooner you'll be able to control that anger before it controls you." That was real good advice; he knew, because he lived through it himself. But I "really" had a hard time with anger, and hating certain people.

You know how you can be walking along and all of a sudden the Great Eagle of Wisdom shits in your mess gear (you know, something you can't ignore)? Well, it was like that for me one day when I decided to take in a movie at a cheap little theater near where I lived. The name of this movie was "Barfly," and I think Faye Dunaway and Mickey Rourke played the main roles (sorry folks, if that's not exact; brain is firing at max. output). Anyway, I needed a break, movies seemed to work, and there was no old Jar Head giving me a heads up on anything like I'm tryin' to do for you.

So I sprayed on some flea repellent, bought a dollar ticket, walked in and took a seat at the back of the theater; good field of fire, no one can sneak up on ya. The movie kind of reminded me of a few bad times in my own life, so I wasn't feeling real warm and tingly. But it was only a buck for an hour and a half of therapy. Beats the hell out 100 bucks an hour. Anyway, there I was killing a little time.

And then it happened! I could feel the "swirl" of the Eagle's Wing, and the scent of victory approach. (it was probably the air conditioner kickin' on and the old sandwich under the seat)! In this movie, someone says to Rourke, "Man, don't you just hate that guy?" and Rourke replies:

"No, I don't hate him, I just feel better when he's not around."

And with that one comment, the light went on in my small green brain!

So I stopped hating all the assholes in my life that day. This instantly saved great sums of money for ammo. And I also stopped pretending that I fit into their "Little Things" world. This not only made me more wealthy, it also relieved me of constantly being pissed off and feeling responsible for flushing the toilet of humanity. And guess what? I did feel better when they " weren't around," and I felt better about myself as well. Of course, after awhile, I found other

19

members of the "I Don't Give A Shit Club." But for a time, it just felt better to be alone, and not around people that made me feel guilty for not being like them. It was sorta' like a praying mantis pretending to be a cockroach.

Just like all of you young Warriors comin' back today, my reality had changed; my life had changed, and I didn't even know it. Our war experiences force us into a deeper understanding of what "truly" is important, at least for us. But don't feel alone on this one. Every other Vet I know feels exactly the same way. I learned that first hand, at a Veteran's Outreach Center back in the early 80's. We'll cover that topic later on.

In this "Guide," I'm making a 100% effort to cover all the possible feelings you might be having, and addressing all the "crazy" thoughts you may be thinking. It's also very important that I clear up, or at least explain some things that you may be judging yourself over. If no one ever talks to you about some of this stuff, how are you ever gonna figure out if you really are a few cans short of a six pack, or you've just had some really unusual experiences (or both)?

Now, I heard a few assholes snap shut when I mentioned the Angel of Death, so before we move on to the next topic, I want to shed some light on this Beautiful Being.

It has been said that "there are no disbelievers in the foxhole," and I sure as hell believe in a God, and I definitely believe in the Angel of Death.

"Oh, here we go," you say?

Well, don't go after the keys to the padded cell just yet. Hear me out first, then decide.

In war, on the battlefield, with all the death and suffering, there is a powerful, calm presence that charges the air with a feeling of expectation. It's a little un-nerving at first, because you can actually feel the energy of this Angel as she approaches. And yes, to me the Angel of Death is in the form of a magnificent, beautiful woman, with piercing blue eyes, and jet black hair, tall and perfectly proportioned. How do I know what she looks like? Use your imagination again.

And I'm sure she looks different to everyone, but from

the studies I've done on Her since the war, she appears mostly as a woman, and some have even discovered one of Her names. It is Miriam. The Angel of Death is not that dipshit, hooded bag of bones with a scythe. Best as I can tell, that was dreamed up by some monk on a bad batch of mushrooms, to scare the hell out of a bunch of folks livin' around a castle.

Make no mistake about Her, however. When She approaches, the air is so charged that the hair on the back of your neck stands straight out, and you feel both a longing and a fear at the same time. Maybe the longing is our feeling of wanting to get off of this rock, and back to the Big Base Camp in the Sky? And maybe the fear is simply being next to something, or someone, so powerful? Don't know, just a best guess.

But what I do know, is that when your time is up, She is right there. How do I know this? Well, it's because I've seen, and been around a lot of Death, and every single time, at that moment, if you pay attention, you can feel Her presence.

The first time this happened, I was standing watch the night before a major operation, being entertained by the monkeys that seemed to take great pleasure out of rattling the cans on our barbed wire and scaring the shit out of us. Anyway, I was thinking about the next day, and I started to feel like someone was standing in back of me. You develop a sixth sense after a short time in a war; you know when you are being watched.

And after a long time, you can even tell if its animal or human, and in what direction the stare is coming from.

Since I was surrounded by Marines and feeling very safe, I just turned around to be my usual smart ass self, but no one was there! Then I felt Her Energy! The hair stood up on the back of my neck, and I saw a picture of my best friend standing beside her. He and I were close friends on the high school football team, and had joined the Corps together, gone through the same platoon in boot camp, and were in the same unit in Nam. Thinking "What the Hell is going on?,' I quickly lit up a cigarette, and another, and another until my watch was over.

A few days later, I said goodbye to my brother for the

last time. He was a rifleman same as me, and was killed by a sniper a few feet from my position. Coincidence you say? I might agree with you, except that isn't the only time it happened.

After a few months, it became the norm when "She" would hang out with the troops. Maybe She always did, and we just didn't know it. By the way, I wasn't the only one thinkin' this was the most beautiful round-eye I'd ever seen.

Eventually, it got so comfortable that I looked forward to Her presence. It was such a terrible time, I suppose I was hoping She had come for me; guess I had to stick around to watch your 6:00 o'clock.

Look, I'm not sayin' that I took long hot showers with the Angel of Death. What I am saying is that She is real, and commands a hell of lot of respect. Each time I' d feel that energy, I would always bow my head and maintain a humble posture. You know, as a reverent greeting to a powerful individual. I could tell you more about this from what I've learned over the years since the war, but suffice it to say, that this beautiful Angel is someone to look forward to, and not to be feared. Her special gift for everyone is taking each of us back to the Prime Source, back to God, and what could be better than that?

So then, in case some of you Youngins have felt any of the same things about Miriam, remember the Old Sarge. You ain't crazy, and neither am I on this one. And you also need to keep in mind, that the only problem you really have, is being a "decent human being." This is as true as a sighted in Model 700 (Sniper rifle). Think about it, and once again, cut yourself some slack.

Now, grab your gear, we're movin' out again. And **"Fix Bayonets!"** It's "hand to hand", "hookin' and jabbin" on this next topic. Stay by my side! We may need to go back-to-back on this one!

1-5 A Warrior's Job is to Kill

Every day that I went on patrol, which was a lot, our orders were to engage and destroy. And every time we'd meet the enemy, which was a lot, we'd kill as many of them as "we" could, and they'd kill as many of us as "they" could. After a firefight, we'd tend to the dead, chopper them and the severely wounded out, then head back to base, or continue with the operation. This is the life of a Warrior. You fight until you die, get wounded, or go home. Just that simple.

Thinking that I understood this Warrior concept, I joined the Marine Corps, one week after my 17th birthday. And, being a simple, dumb-ass-boot at the time, I actually thought I'd finally found my calling and a real home in the Corps. At the time, I even thought of being a lifer (stayin' in for 20+). Over the course of Boot Camp, Rifleman's Training, and Guerilla Warfare School, my young civilian ass was transformed into a well-trained killer. That was the sole purpose of my existence: to think like the enemy, to find the enemy, and to kill the enemy in an open firefight, or wherever he was hiding.

Regardless of what branch of the Ground Forces you're in, a grunt's job is the same. You're a Warrior, and Warriors fight wars. By the way, the term "grunt" is what we called a basic ass-in-the-grass Marine rifleman, in a line company, in a fire team, (M.O.S. 0311). You know, a ground-pounder. Although all Marines go through most of the same training to a point, the grunts in the line companies do most of the day-in day-out fighting. At least that's how it used to be.

Now, the Marine Corps didn't lie to me, did an excellent job in training me, and certainly instilled a sense of pride and honor that I still carry today. But, at least in those days, they never prepared us for the "emotional battleground" that all combat Vets experience. Actually, in all fairness to the military in general, I really believe that the whole social revolution thing in the 60's and 70's pushed most of us over the edge, and not **completely** the war experiences. So you'd have to cut the Pentagon some slack. If they didn't have to deal with so many politicians, their job would run a lot smoother.

I'll explain what I mean by it not being the military's

fault, because I believe it's very important for Americans now to understand what happened then.

At least at the present time, it appears that the attitude toward our young warriors is a "positive one," and I want to make sure it stays that way. It's critical that all Americans don't treat our new Veterans like they treated us. So let's take a short run back and see what happened.

If you talk with any of the remaining World War II Veterans, and then Korean War Veterans, you'll notice that there is truly a big difference between their attitudes and the attitudes of a Vietnam Vet. I've talked with many from each group, and the difference is striking. Why so you ask? Look...I'm not a history freak, or one of those folks that gets their jollies by figuring out why a whole society goes down the shit tube. I'm just an old Sarge that's talked to a lot of Warriors, and "walked the walk" myself. So take it for what it's worth.

If you think about it, what was the one difference in all three of these major wars? The warriors all fought with honor, kicked ass on the enemy and came home. All of the ones who actually did the fighting sure as hell had traumatic stress disorders. That is, if they were human, they had'em. If you've noticed, even the old WW II Vets still cry on TV when they recall experiences back some 60 years ago. I'll explain just why this happens later on. And every single Combat Vet had to go through the same process in order to get back to some kind of a life in society.

Having said that, now let's look at the "Attitudes" of the American people and the "Attitudes" of the returning Veterans. First off, Hitler was an asshole, and invaded Europe, Japan bombed Pearl Harbor and who knows what Mussolini was thinkin'. They were all good reasons to go to war. And everyone in this country not only agreed that war was necessary, they also got behind the troops. "Our Troops" were all heroes, and the country, hell, a good part of the world, loved America, and loved her military. They should, because if weren't for us, they'd still be high- steppin' to the market, the Mercedes plant, or around the Eiffel Tower.

But things started to backslide a little in Korea. First of all, the government called that "war" a Police Action. What cake-eatin', soft-body, shit-for-brains politician would call a war a Police Action? A police action is a drug bust on maggot-dope-heads, or in military terms, picking up garbage and cleaning up the squad bay. It is not hand-to-hand combat in frozen, blood soaked mountains, with the commies attacking in human waves.

To me, Korea was an example of the worst possible conditions a war could be fought in. And yet, once again, our warriors kicked some communist ass, established a pro-American government, and came home heroes. Maybe they weren't given the parades like the WW II Vets, and maybe they weren't given all the assistance from grateful citizens, but they were still "Respected". You'll have to remember, that the Korean war started only a few years after World War II. People still had the attitude of war in their minds.

Sure, Americans were sick of war, but the communists were out on patrol to take over the world, and had to be stopped. At least, that's what the cake eaters wanted us to believe. Besides, we had to make sure that Korea was a nice safe place for the million-dollar-club CEOs to one day build cars and TV sets for Americans, and the Europeans whose asses we'd just saved.

So when all was said and done, Korean Vets put their nightmares in the closet, didn't talk about their war much (because it wasn't a total "win" like "The Big One") and quietly limped their way through life. Many Americans could sort of sweep Korea under the rug. That way, America's reputation as a real "Kick-your-ass-in-any-war" reputation wasn't hurt so much.

Hello America! Do you see what's coming? I'm just prodding you a bit with the tip of my bayonet. But you sure as hell better not treat our new Veterans like you did the ones 35 to 40 years ago!

And so it was back then, until that unexpected day **"When along came a spider, and sat down beside her:"** a rice propelled, Black Widow in a pointed little hat, to bite America right on the Ass!

There is only one way to describe the Vietnam War. It was a total "Cluster Fuck" in the truest sense of the definition. The Warriors won the battles, and the politicians lost the war; guess they should have never started it. There are plenty of books on the subject, so I'll spare you the details. But let's just focus on the "Troops", and what you ain't gonna do to them again. Right?

Many of the older Vets like myself got sucked into the anti-communist attitude, because Korea hadn't really been over that long, and the Cold War was in full swing. I think that Americans generally felt reluctant to get into another war so soon, but went along with the cake-eaters on this one, and as usual, really gave their power away to the Caribbean Junket Club.

So then, there we were in a war, as an occupation force, trying to make another global market place. You know, a one-stop-shopping-center like Korea. Trouble was, and you could hear the whining all the way from Washington, "but it's not working like Korea!" and "Oh shit, what do we do?"

Maybe I should I have used the spelling "butt"? You know like in butt-fucked? Because that was exactly what was about to happened to America, and all of Her Young Warrior Children. It didn't take long for the country to become politically divided, even worse than it is now. And as the Civil Rights movement and the Anti-War Movement gained momentum, it was like a 28 inch Katanna Sword cutting through a watermelon. The country basically split into two sides. In the one camp were the anti-government troops, symbolically represented by long hair, peace signs, and the "We're taken back our power" mentality. In the other camp, were the pro-corporations, the pro-war-hawkpoliticians, and the high ranking, desperate for "victory" military.

Unfortunately, "All" the military personnel became the scapegoat (or should I say, goat-fucked) symbol for every anti-war clan. And this brings me to the point. For our down-in-the -trenches, blood-covered-soul troops, this wasn't like any other war in American History. The news media made things even worse. Supposedly the "Watchdogs of Freedom", they plastered every single event, every single riot, and every war scene on the evening news, adding fuel to a fire that already had the intensity of a napalm strike. And when the warriors returned Stateside, they were caught right in the middle of it!

Get this straight America! Iraq is **not** Arabic for Vietnam! Don't make it that!

This time let's keep welcoming our troops back with open arms and open hearts, get them the help they need, and do not repeat old mistakes. And let's face one fact squarely: the damage is **already done** for our troops in Afghanistan and Iraq, with at least 250 thousand (maybe more than twice that number) American men and women **now** with a traumatic stress disorder.

This time, let's take care of America's Youth, not sweep their problems under the carpet, and treat every one of them as if they were our own children. They have enough to deal with, and don't need any more stress in their lives. Just because the war ends, doesn't mean the Post Traumatic Stress they're living with ends as well. That baggage stays with them for the rest of their lives. I can vouch for that.

Now, once again, a **"Warrior's job is to kill!"** Of course that's not all they do, no shit. I'm just focusing on that particular skill, because it's the one that's doin' most of the damage. Even back when I put on my uniform for the first time, if someone would have asked me "are you prepared to kill human beings?" I would have said "Yes Sir!", being totally unaware of the consequences at the time. And as many of you now know, once you pull that trigger, "There ain't no taken it back!"

Taking a human life, in a mild sense, creates the same kind of helpless feeling as when someone gets caught cheating on a spouse, or when the Judge slams that hammer down on your ass, and locks you up for 10 years. You say "Oh Shit! I can't get out of this," it's final! Same-e-Same. Talking to some of our Young Vets, I realized that they are just like I was. Hell, I thought I was killing a "Commie for Christ"; they believe they're fighting to stop terrorism. Not much difference in this old green brain. Thing is, you "Youngins" are a lot smarter than I ever was, and you have a better idea of what's goin' on in the world. I never had a clue.

But I'm here to tell you Warriors, it's not your fault for gettin' sucked into the "It's an Adventure Club", the "Be all you can be", or one of "A few good men". I'm sure the recruiter never mentioned how you'd pay the ultimate price, whether you got wasted or not.

One last point, then we'll move on to higher ground. Always better to be shootin' down-hill. First of all, you **are** a

Warrior, you **are** killing people, and you don't feel good about it. Here's your wakeup call!

You don't have to feel good about it, you just have to do it, and you had better do a damn good job of it as well, like it or not. If you hesitate to pull that trigger, either you or your friends are gonna' end up in a body bag. Do whatever you have to do, and when your hitch is up, then you will have the liberty to decide, if you want to keep doin' it.

When all the killing is over, chances are real good you're gonna' have a jammed round in your brain-housing-group, and without some help, you're gonna' have a hell of a time gettin' it out.

Now listen up! It doesn't make you a bad Soldier or Marine to admit that you feel emotions. No shit, I've know men who were stone cold killers, no feelings, no guilt, no remorse what-so-ever. I think that in any war, most of us go through a period like that, you just don't want to stay there. You see my friends, at that point, killing becomes cold blooded murder. And you don't want to end up in a Federal Prison with your cell mate introducing you as his bitch.

As for you civilians out there, like it or not, **if** you've been through anything like the shit-bath I've been talkin' about, you've just joined the Brother-Sisterhood of the marginally insane. It's not so bad though, we're all here to back you up! And you'd be surprised at how big the roster is and who's on it.

OK, now let's head over to a new HOT L.Z!

Door gunners at the ready!

1-6 Hardening to Loss

There are several issues here to consider , and we'll address each one. This was a very difficult problem for me, as well as many of my fellow Vets from Vietnam. I suspect some aspects of loss are timeless, and many of you Young Warriors will know exactly what I'm explaining here.

It's a little different now with the wars in Afghanistan and Iraq, since a lot of units travel together. In some ways, it can be worse than the single rotation policy of the Nam because the feelings of loss are greater with long term associations.

First let's deal with the fact that we've lost "true friends". In the civilian world, such comparisons are paralled by partnerships in police units, firefighters, emergency services, or any other high risk units where trust is critical. In a life and death situation, where you know that your friend will literally die protecting you, a bond of Brother/Sisterhood develops that goes beyond words. You love these individuals with all your heart, and are willing to give up your own life to protect theirs.

In my own experiences I have lost many of my beloved brothers, killed in the heat of a firefight, right in front of me. I know what it feels like: the rage, the desire for revenge, the pain in your chest that feels like your heart has just been ripped out from your rib cage. Then, when it's all over, and the body bags are loaded on the choppers with all that remains of the best friends you've ever had, you feel the deepest sense of helplessness and loss imaginable.

Brace yourself, because the feelings of loss "never completely go away." They just get a lot more bearable with time, and eventually, go to a place in your mind, where you mostly remember the laughter, and the good times in your life that you've shared with these true friends, and not just when their lives ended. This is a hard one to deal with, but you **can** do it, and you don't have to do it alone.

Let's talk about that a bit. And remember, the way you deal with this issue is a custom fit in many ways, but there are some common tactics that will help everyone. There is a saying I heard, and I don't know exactly who said it (don't really care), but it goes something like this:

"Courage my friend, and greet the unseen with a cheer, for there are no worse things to be gone through, than men (women) have gone before, and by my troth I care not, so let go which way it will, for a man (woman) can die but once."

I heard this "in country", and even though it's not real cheery, somehow it seemed to help a little. Made me think that no matter how bad I had it, some Warrior in the past had it just as bad or worse.

But here's one of the hard parts. You know by now that the pain of loss comes in "Waves". Something you see, hear, or think about can trigger the next wave. Your mind can, and does, bring you back to any place or time in your association with your dead friend, and starts replaying the whole thing from that point.

At first, it's like an endless loop that only seems to play the most painful parts of the movie. However, each time the "Wave" is over, the next wave will not be as difficult, not be quite so intense. This is how it works for most of us. Why does it work that way, you ask? Well, I can only tell you how it's worked for me, and other Vets, and why the grieving process works like it does for us Warriors.

Sometimes you may feel a little guilty, because you don't want to forget your best friends, but thinking about them causes you intense pain. This is like a Catch-22, you know, being caught between a rock and a hard place. Don't worry about feeling guilty, but **do not** try to ignore the feelings and waves that are pounding you from the actual death of your friend. I tried to ignore it, tried to drink it away, and it only prolongs the "intensity" of each cycle.

Each time you face the wave head on, you begin to **accept** the event of death a little more. The best example I can think of is surfing. When you're paddling out in the surf, and a large set of waves is approaching, if you roll over, flipping under your board (use to call that "turtling") the wave goes right over you, and the board takes the pounding. If you stay on top of the surfboard, you get your ass kicked by Kahuna. Ignoring the fact that your friends are dead and you can't do a damn thing about it, or for some other reason, like survivor guilt, you may feel the need to punish yourself, by staying on top of the board.

Each time you accept the death of your friends and begin to remember the good times, and being glad you could spend some quality time with some quality people, you are turtling under the wave of emotion. You are then forming a new habit, a new way of thinking. And each time it hurts a little bit less. What I'm saying here is, by the act of accepting the event, you are allowing yourself to look at it in a less destructive way. And the waves become smaller and smaller each time you do. This does seem to work for many of us.

So each time you remember your dead friends, the thoughts are of the good times you shared. It took me a long time and many bottles of wine to begin to understand this. Finally, with the help of the VA counselors, and less wine, it all made sense, and I started turtling.

"How long will it take to learn to turtle?" That, my friends, depends on how honest you are with yourselves, and how many other issues are clinging to the turtle's back. You see, that's the big problem with War Veterans. It isn't just one issue at a time. In Section Five: topic 5-3, Why Do I Have PTSD? I've listed a whole smorgasbord of crusty little, barnacle-like symptoms to stick on your nice smooth shell. The good news is that once you start to constructively deal with loss, it moves quickly to **an acceptable level of discomfort**. It took me about a year, with survivor guilt stuck to my shell. Some Vets got through it in months. After several years, it really is very manageable, and like I said, you'll never forget the best friends you've ever had, and you shouldn't!

As a suggestion, while the waves are intense, watching the news at night doesn't help at all. Anything that rekindles the emotions starts the waves again. Every time I'd get a letter from a buddy that informed me of yet another friend being killed, I'd drop right back into the pit, into a good drunk. After a time, I just couldn't face it anymore, and stopped opening letters. Sounds like a shithead approach, but at the time, I was alone and trying to survive. I just didn't know how else to deal with it. Sometimes, you get backed into a corner, and you don't think you can stand one more lump of shit falling from the sky.

On a lighter note, someone once told me, that "just

31

because the phone rings, doesn't mean you have to answer it." I'm sure there's a deeper meaning to this, but to my simple way of thinking, it meant, pull the plug on the TV, cut the phone line, and carry an umbrella when you walk under a tree. Don't make your life more miserable than it has to be. Remember my friends: **you are not alone!** And I'm gonna keep sayin' that until you hear it in your sleep. Oh, and by the way, once you do get some of this trauma crap in the right place in your head, you **will** be able to sleep without nightmares. Just thought I throw that in. And you sure as hell won't need any help from that creepy little alien moth shitting on your forehead to help you do it.

There are a few ways to start to deal with the first sets of waves, without the use of Zombie meds (tried those too). If you're a light drinker, you can allow yourself "one" good drunk in the company of other Vets or a true friend that's had "similar experiences." That is, not alone or behind the wheel of a car or a motorcycle. Why, you ask? Because you may decide the pain is too much in the beginning, and kill yourself. Remember, you're dealing with multiple problems.

I've lost many of my V.A. buddies this way. They couldn't deal with the pain, and couldn't find someone with "like experiences" to talk with as the wave hit. Their solution was to drive off a cliff, cross the center line, or stick a shotgun in their mouth and pulled the trigger. This is not the way to solve your problems! And why do I keep saying "like experience"? Because no one will have a clue about what you're feeling, unless they've been down the same road you have, and feel the same way.

I'm not a bean-counter-war-history kinda person, but I do recall that in Vietnam, we lost about 50 thousand troops in combat. We lost about 48 thousand to suicide. That ain't no small number, and us Old Timers wanna make sure that doesn't happen again. Any suicide is a needless waste of life. I'll go over that topic in detail when we come to Section Four.

"So what do I do after the binge?" you ask. Well, you sober up, have another good cry, be grateful you're alive, and get on with life. That's right, I said cry! Men do cry. I have, and so have the bravest, fiercest Warriors I've ever known. There is no shame in feeling, and no shame in letting

32

those feelings out. You may as well do it now, cause it's gonna come back around to bite you on the ass later.

If you can't find a real friend who's been down the same road as you, then think of something that just might make you feel better, and **force** yourself to do it. I use to like a long motorcycle ride, until my ass was numb, then I'd stop for a real meal at some greasy spoon. Maybe a movie works for you, or a trip to the zoo or the aquarium. Hell, maybe a tank of fish, or an active hobby or sport. You just don't want to be sitting on your ass, staring at the walls when the waves are coming. It makes you drink more, and that makes you more depressed. Been there, done that.

Sometimes I'd grab a couple of bottles (air bottles), go out to the kelp beds, and go for a dive. I'd just sit on the bottom, feeding fish with urchins until the air would run out. Sometimes I'd go down to the docks, and listen to "Lights Out Jazz'" at one of the night clubs down in San Diego. It's whatever gives you a little peace and increases the distance between the waves of grief.

If you feel angry like I did, I'd go down to the rifle range, and without ear plugs, crank off two magazines of .308 in my M-14, pulling the trigger as fast as I could. This show of fire-power seemed to amaze some of the wide-eyed spectators, and there were always some who would take a few paces back as I returned to my bike. But "I didn't give a shit," and firing "my girl" (called her Raptor) made me feel better.

Mindless driving is another thing that often helped. I'm not sure if it was because I'm a Marine, or if it just gives you a chance to be active and not think about "too" much at the same time. Of course I'm not saying to go to sleep at the wheel! I'm just sayin' that driving can sometimes help. You know, going on a trip to a nice place?

Just remember, to allow yourself to feel, to go through the grieving process. And "Damn it!" remember, "This is how you're suppose to react!" **There is nothing wrong with you.** There is nothing wrong with feeling devastated by the loss of someone you loved.

"One Day at a time, One Wave at a time,"

33

and be glad you're alive, with your "Life" ahead of you. It can only get better when you're at the bottom of the pit!

Hold on to that thought! We're headin' into another Hot L.Z ! (Landing Zone)

Keep reading. You don't have to like it, you just have to do it!

1-7 Friendship and Survivor Guilt

In the civilian world, the term "friend" is often used casually, and without a lot of concern over just what that actually means. I always get a chuckle inside, when someone says to me, "Oh, you just have to meet my friends." In my mind, I see a fire team of combat hardened Warriors, dripping with sweat, loaded down with weapons and ammo, at the ready to kill to protect each other. And when I have "Met the Friends," more often than not, it was a bunch of vitamin-poppin-limp-dicks that couldn't figure out which pair of nikes went best with their BMW.

If you look in the "Big Book of Words" (that's what Marines call the Dictionary), the word friend means comrade, someone you like, or trust. Well that's OK for the "nike club," but for us warriors, that "Don't quite get it". And you know what I'm talkin' about. To us, a friend is to be trusted with your life. He or she is always your back up, always watchin' your 6 O'clock, always there if you need someone on your flank; you know, like the wing man on Top Gun, or ridin' shotgun. Same-e-Same.

The first time I was in a fire fight, surrounded by the "Little People," and my brothers and I were back to back, I learned what trust was; no little rice-propelled warrior in black pajamas was sneakin' up on me without having field surgery on the spot. That is, a new asshole placed in the middle of his head. My brothers, my "friends," protected me with their lives, and I returned the privilege of putting my life on the line for them. You don't get any closer than that.

This is the way it's always been with Warriors, and **that's the way it is today!** With Warriors, the bond of true friendship is developed, tested, sealed in trust, and cherished as the result of any war, or life and death conflict. When you go into battle together, you do so with "friends" you can "trust." And when every battle is over, once again, you look at "life" and true "friendship" a whole lot differently.

The more conflicts you live through together, the stronger the bond of friendship, and the mutual love between you. Yeah! That's right, I said Love! Remember, as a human being, you're suppose to "feel" emotions? Now I'm not talking about the ooey-gooey, sloppy, kissy-in-the-shower love. I'm talkin' about honorable, respectful, "Somebody-just-saved-your-ass and you owe'm love."

"So what's the problem," you ask? Real simple. What happens when the friend you love gets wasted (killed), and you don't. And even worse, what happens if this is repeated over and over again? And worse again, what happens if you never even get a scratch, while what's left of your "friends" are being scraped up off the ground and choppered out in half a body bag?

This repeated event starts to eat at you like a pack of wolves on a fresh kill. You think to yourself, " Why didn't I step on that land mine?", "Why wasn't I killed?", and "What the hell is going on here?" Every one of these self-destructive, cancerous thoughts stays locked in your brain-housing- group adding to the growing catalog of nightmares each time you fall asleep.

After a time of repeated "loss," mounting survivor guilt, and being a part of, or witness to, continual killing, you become closed off, numb, and even a little reckless at times. I'll give you a couple of examples. And by the way, my Young Warrior Friends, I'm only telling you all this so that just maybe you can identify with the feelings taking place. And maybe you'll have a heads-up in advance, so you won't do what I did.

About 11 months into my 13 month tour (Marine Corps had to one-up the Army by a month) I was one of the coldest sons of bitches on the planet. After the loss of the best high school friend of my life, and I'd just as soon not say how many true friends I also lost in the war, I wanted revenge, and I didn't give a shit if I lived or died in the process. I know, that some of you feel the same way, right now. That's why some of you, in some ways, don't mind going back to the wars in Afghanistan and Iraq for a second tour (or more). Your "friends" are there, and you can't stand the thought of not covering their backs. This driving force "to be with your fellow Warriors" goes beyond family ties, beyond patriotism, or just plain common sense. And sometimes, it's survivor guilt that makes you decide to return to war, or to be reckless in it. I'll give you an example.

We were on one of our typical operations, burning everything in our path, taking prisoners for interrogation, and killing everyone who resisted. We came into a clearing and in the center of it was an old church, all blown to hell, but the tower was still pretty much intact.

I was part of a small group of Marines running the flank position, to make sure the main unit didn't get ambushed. As soon as we moved into the clearing and near the church, we started taking fire from a few Viet Cong, trying to make their way to the river. Thanks to the bullshit Geneva Convention, this was a river we couldn't cross, and there weren't any Korean Marines around to help out. They didn't need to follow the "so called" Rules of War. They did what the hell needed to be done, no questions asked.

Feeling a lot of survivor guilt, and not giving a shit, I climbed up on the tower, and started trying to kill as many of the enemy as I could. Well, not all the Cong had made it to the river yet. They saw me, and I saw them, and we all got into a great little fire fight. As the Marines down on the ground began to charge the Cong under fire (no small thing to do), I kept trying to keep the enemy on the run. After it was over, and with my rifle smoking like bratwurst on a grill, I stopped and looked at where I was standing.

During the battle, the names of all my dead brothers were rolling through my brain. All I could do was fire, and think "this one's for Bob, this one's for Dennis, this one's for Sgt Mac!" I was in a blind rage, with no thought whatsoever for my own safety. A Marine sergeant had also climbed up during the firefight to be my spotter, as I was trying to kill the Cong crossing the river. He looked at me, and looked at the wall where I was standing and said, "Holy fuck, Brandi, look at this shit!" I was completely covered with plaster, and enemy rounds had hit everywhere around my body except where I was standing, forming a silhouette of sorts. Now you may think this was a real good thing, but I didn't. It only made me feel even more guilty, because once again, I didn't get hit! This kind of experience actually increases survivor guilt and encourages recklessness, even thoughts of suicide by way of battle. And no shit, my own survivor guilt increased even more.

The same kind of situation happened one more time while we were trying to med-evac our wounded, and I became even more careless with my own life. That is, until I came close the end of my 13 month tour, when a little girl looked into my soul and made me realize what a monster I'd become. I'll tell you about that in the next topic.

So what do you do about "Survivor Guilt?"

"YOU SURVIVE!"

It's just that simple. You don't dishonor the friends who died to protect you. You remember the good times you shared, and the bonds of real friendship that will guide for you for the rest of your life. Think about it! **If they thought you were worth dying for, don't you think you're worth living for?** I sure as hell do.

After 40 years, I still see the faces of my Brothers, smiling, laughing, and encouraging me to go on; to push forward, do something useful with my life, and have a damn good time doing it.

So to you young warriors, I'm saying, **"Use the friendships of "trust" and "honor" as your standard, and your standard is excellence!** We'll talk about where to get some help with this trauma in a bit.

Now, let's break camp, and get back in the bush. We've got a ways to go, and it's easier to see the booby traps in daylight.

Why do you think the head-shrinkers use to call a traumatic stress disorder Battle Fatigue? In their small, cluttered, pencil-pushin' minds, all they could figure out was that "Gee whiz!", I guess this warrior is gettin' burned out from being shot at, killing women and children, going without sleep, watching his friends getting wasted, and having everybody with a pointed hat (now a Pizza Hut table cloth) on their heads trying to kill him. Well no shit Sherlock! Talk about no-brainers!

At a certain point in every Warrior's tour, no matter how hard you try to suppress it, you simply get overwhelmed. The more combat you're in and the more killing you do, the sooner it happens. If you get too burned out too soon, then chances are you're gonna "Screw the Pooch." You know, make a mistake, not stay focused, and get yourself or someone else killed. Fortunately, burn-out usually doesn't become a disabling problem until you realize you're gettin' close to the end of your tour.

Most of the Combat Vets I know don't watch the ambulance-chasing nightly news, except maybe to get a guess-timation update from the crap-shoot weather reports. Sometimes however, I can stomach PBS only because Jim Lehrer is a brother Marine. He says things the way they are. And it was on one such night not so long ago that I saw something that made me a little un-easy.

Of course, most of the channels milk the Iraq war, to get the last drop of blood on the screen for their ratings, (ever wonder what happened to Afghanistan?), but this night, they were interviewing some beady-eyed politician. He was explaining how it was just decided by him and other members of his colony to extend the tours of several combat units near Baghdad, by six months!

My stomach turned as I listened, but there was no way I could reach his lily-white, pencil-neck through the TV screen. This man had no clue about what he had just done. Of course, he "acted" concerned; most good actors can change from laughter to tears in the same sentence, and man, you gotta think about those votes! Then he went on to say, how "there was just no choice," and the troops were gonna' "simply (?) have to tuff it out," as he wiped the grease from his chin and whiskers after that tasty gourmet lunch at the Hilton.

I know how important it is to **think** you're comin' home, and I know full well what an order like that can do to morale. There were a lot of men and women markin' off the days until they were headin' back to the land of the big PX (Post Exchange). It's like being on death row, and having someone move up your execution date, or like thinking you're cured of cancer, and having it come back.

A year tour can feel like a lifetime. It's a little different for everyone, but by about six months or so "in country" you've made some kind of a mental transition. Where you are, seems like where you've always been. In about the middle of the tour, you've learned the customs and adapted your skills as a Warrior in order to survive, or by that time, you'd likely be dead or wounded. It's also a point of acceptance. That is, you're there, making the best of it, and you've just got too damn long to go before leaving. And yet, in the back of your mind, you remember that somewhere over the Big Pond, there's a place with Golden Arches and an artery clogging meal just waiting with your name on it.

Mid-tour is kind of a strange place to be. You can't think about how long you've been there, because it makes you dread the idea of how long you have to go. And folks, this ain't like some nice, cozy vacation spot in the Bahamas. Besides thinkin' about how long you've got left, you're also sweatin' whether you'll be walking to the airport, or being carried in a body bag; you're dealing with **all** the traumatic stresses of war.

There is, however, an up-side to this rock and a hard place position you find yourself in, well, sort of. It's called humor. Now, as you might suspect, on the battlefield, in a war, its gonna' be "graveyard" humor. Here, let me give you an example of how little things can be amusing in a twisted sort of way.

After a short fire fight one day, we were laying in the mud, by the side of a road. This particular road was bordered on both sides by rice paddies, but high enough to allow us cover, while we waited for the choppers to bring us ammo and take out our wounded. We were dog-ass tired, so after the choppers were loaded, our L T (Lieutenant) told us to take a break, clean our weapons and grab some chow.

In those days, food for the troops came in little boxes called C-rations. There were 12 wonderfully tasty, and unique meals. It was commented on many times by our Marine "taste testers" that these C-rats did indeed taste just like the meals "Mom" use to make, only she didn't shit in'm. Within each box was a main course can, such as spaghetti and meatballs, or beef stew. There were also little cans containing something that resembled bread, or other dessert type substances. And last but not least, was the most wonderful gift of all, an even smaller box, with 5 cigarettes in it. And yes, Uncle Sam, did help to stick the nicotine needle in our arms, compliments of the Good Old Boys in the Southern tobacco plantations. But what the hell did we care. Nobody thought they were comin' home alive anyway.

And there we were, dead tired and watching our wounded being carried off, when one Marine says, "Hey! Look at this shit!" On the side of the mini-pack of cigs was the Surgeon General's warning, "Cigarette smoking can be hazardous to your health." No shit. Well, maybe you had to be there, but we really got a good laugh over that one! A little humor can take your mind off of what you're doing, or what you just did. I don't think I've ever laughed so much in my life as I did with my friends in war. Humor helped smooth out some of the rough times and seemed to make the days pass more quickly.

Maybe the weeks and months did go by slowly, and maybe not, but eventually, the day you were waiting for finally arrived. For most of us, it was the 30 day mark. Then all of a sudden, you begin to think, "Damn! I might just make it out of this shit hole after all!" And that's when it becomes a little more dangerous, especially if you've got a girlfriend or wife that hasn't dumped you yet. You become less anxious to volunteer for extra patrols or operations, and you're carrying a bit more ammo. You're more alert, and a lot more trigger happy. At least I was.

Some of us made "Short timer sticks" to mark off the last few days, and some made their own calendars out of C-rat boxes; back then, real calendars were in short supply. And it's difficult to imagine a more confusing and frustrating time. Yeah, your "friends" are still getting killed and wounded, so might you, but there's now a real glimmer of a chance of making it home.

Well, there I was, still pissed off, and holding on to a very real need to continue killing out of hatred and revenge. And if that weren't bad enough, I had also reached the end of the emotional line. Every single one of the traumatic effects of the war had reached the detonation point. It was like being under a mortar attack with no place to take cover. Anger, hatred, denial, loss, helplessness and guilt, were all hookin-and-jabbin with my brain. And yet, I was about to be sent back into society. I was supposed to be "normal" again?

Scary isn't it? But a lot of warriors were in fact, sent homeward bound with exactly the same state of mind that I'm describing here. And here's another "wake up call" America. **IT'S HAPPENING RIGHT NOW!** These men and women are going through exactly what I did. Going from violent, bloody battles, to a place where no one understands their anger, their resentment, or their need to continue killing to protect their fellow Warriors, or to "settle the score." But like I said, a little girl changed all that for me. Call it blind luck, or call it fate, I don't know. But she and one last patrol changed my life forever.

It was, I recall, after a hearty breakfast of meatballs and canned white bread (with jam) that we left the comfort of our sand-bagged bunker, and took off down the mountain on a pre-dawn patrol. All was quiet, as we walked cautiously along the roads that led through a large expanse of lush, green rice patties. As the sun came up over the horizon, it began to slowly remove some of the threat of a Viet Cong ambush, and we began to relax, just a bit. Most of us were highly "seasoned" Warriors and fully aware of the battle tested routine of a patrol like this one.

It was fully daylight when we came to another large cluster of paddies that we simply could not avoid crossing. One by one, we started out, leaving about 50 meters between each Marine. This was to insure that if we "were" ambushed, everyone wouldn't get pinned down in the same spot, and picked off like in a skeet shoot. It ain't like TV, or some bullshit movie, where you've got twenty guys crammed into the camera's field of view. Like my Old Sarge would say,

"Spread out you assholes, one grenade'll get you all!". True words of wisdom.

About half way across the rice paddy dike, we began to pick up sniper fire from what appeared to be a mud or clay hut, just up ahead. Instantly we returned fire, shooting into the hut, thinking that was the sniper's cover.

Most of the time, it is very difficult to figure out where a single shooter is hiding, unless you can see a muzzle flash, or the bullet striking the ground next to you. That's why the hut seemed like a good bet. But it did seem odd that the sniper wasn't hitting us, the ground, or the water in the rice patty. I remember thinking, "Man! I'm sure glad we ran into a 'retard sniper' that can't shoot for shit on my last patrol!"

Moving in on the hut, the enemy fire suddenly stopped. We were not in the mood to take prisoners that day, and I guarantee you, that if we could have laid our hands on that sniper, he would have helped with the rice harvest, from under the mud.

Two of us reached the door of the hut at the same time, and one Marine went around back to cover the window. Good thing we didn't frag (fragmentary grenade) the hut like we usually did. In a few moments, most of the patrol was covering the hut and us, as we prepared to see what was inside. It was decided that my buddy would kick in the door, and I would be the first to enter. "Right On!" I thought, "My last chance to kill another one of these little bastards before I get out of this shit-hole."

The signal was given, the door was kicked in, and I stepped over the threshold, ready to kill again. But in one revolting gasp, all I can remember saying is "Oh God! Forgive me!" then, "God Damn this fucking place!"

Like I said, we were all hardened, combat Warriors, but in one fleeting instant, we were brought to our knees. As I stared around the room, as we all stared around the room, what looked back at us was the most beautiful group of children I'd ever seen. Beautiful that is, except for the gaping rips in their flesh, now peeled back on their delicate little bodies. Wounds made by our rounds!

I slung my rifle over my shoulder, and reached down to a little girl whose eyes hadn't left mine from the time I'd stepped into the room. She held one arm up to me, as I asked

God to "Please forgive me, for such a horrible mistake, for causing children to suffer in this unforgivable way." I picked this little one up, and her eyes were dark as night. I pressed her close, and she smiled at me. My God, she just smiled at me, after what I had done!

A round had entered her body at two points, and the flesh on both her arm and leg was peeled back almost to the bone. Yet she never said a word, she just stared into my eyes, and smiled with the kindest expression I had ever seen. As she clung to my neck, I could feel the warmth of her small body. The reality of this moment had pierced my soul, like the kindness from her eyes. At least for a time, the hate had ended, and the revenge was over. Perhaps for the first time, I had realized, there truly is no difference between any of us.

Long after my arms were numb from her weight, and my clothes and body soaked from her blood, I carried her on, not thinking or caring about the war, about the enemy, or about life itself. All I wanted to do was to get this gentle little child to a chopper pad, to be med-evaced out. I did just that.

My friends, I fell in love with the human race that day. In love with the strength and dignity of the human spirit, and it took a child to show me the way. Her beautiful dark eyes will be in my memory, and in my heart, for life. Something like this makes you love the potential of every child, for what they might one day become. Being even more confused and shocked from this last experience, the only clear priority I had left was to get myself the hell out of a war zone, and I didn't have to wait too long for that to happen.

In the final days before the big extraction, we all became a little more confident, and I'm sure a lot more irritating to be around, especially to the new guys. We'd sit around firing down brain-grenades (beers) and everyone had their fantasies about "the first thing they'd do when they got stateside!" I'd imagine it's the same now, and the dreams as well. When you were allowed to sleep, the dreams were so real, that is was a shock to wake up "in country." You'd swear you were actually in your dreams.

So there we were, just like you warriors today, never suspecting the ambush just up ahead. The thought never occurred to us that "we" had a problem. To us, the only problem was the war. We thought " everything will be back to normal, as soon as I get home," and "It will all be over." Does this sound a little familiar?

Finally the day arrives. You've made it! Only one more ride to the airport. And man, I'll never forget that ride. My asshole was puckered tight. I saw a land mine under every bump, an ambush at every corner, but somehow we finally managed to make it to that airport.

My trip to Vietnam was on a military, C-130 prop-transport, out of Okinawa. But when I came back, it was cruisin' in style with Continental Airlines, a jet propelled aircraft, with beautiful round- eyed women. I still remember the flight back. All I kept thinking was " I made it! Thank you God. I'm goin home."

But circling the LAX airport before landing, this unsettling feeling came over me, kept warning me, "Something's not right down there." I was confused, because it felt just like when you're expecting the enemy to show up. "How can this be?" I thought.

But little did I know, that another war was about to begin, a war that could take my life as quickly as an AK-47.

Here we go, my young Brothers and Sisters. Stay alert!

We're headin' into that ambush we never expected!

Section One Summary

1-1 The Death of Innocence

- The war changed your life forever.

- There's nothing wrong with your feelings; you are supposed to feel emotions.

- It's going to take some time, and help, for you to feel better.

- You have the strength of a Warrior. You can do it, so cut yourself some slack.

1-2 From Videos to Killing Kids

- Only other combat Vets will understand what you are feeling. Only those with like experiences will have a clue what you're talking about. Don't waste your time with those who don't. It will just frustrate you more.

- Parents, old friends, or family members who have not shared your same experiences will not understand you. Find other Combat Vets, or someone that will.

- You will need some alone time to process your thoughts. Check out the Veterans Outreach Center in your area, for some friendlies.

- Surrender is not in your Creed.

1-3 Taking Life, Changes Life

- You will never be the same person you were, so get on with making a new "Life Plan".

- You are not alone! All of us old warriors are with you, watchin' your 6 o'clock.

- You fit in somewhere, just decide where that is, and start working' on it.

- You're going to change civilian friends, maybe you'll have to re-think family, or maybe you'll just need to live alone.

- Whatever you decide, is the right thing for you. You've earned it. Start feeling comfortable with not trying to fit into every one's expectations of how you should be. Just be you.

- You are a good Human Being, or you wouldn't feel squat shit. Start "feeling" your way into your new life, your new future.

1-4 What is Reality?

- You are not like everyone else. You never will be. So deal with it! Get on with your new "Life Plan".

- Plan your future, but live one day at a time. It's all you really have.

- "Don't sweat the little things, and if it's not life threatening, it's a little thing!"

- Remember, the "I don't give a shit" attitude. It will help you with the "little things"

- It hurts to be rejected; it feels good to be accepted. Find other people who accept you, and start feeling good about you.

- Don't hate'em, just feel better when they're not around.

- The only problem you have, is being a Human Being. That's Good! Feeling good about yourself, is good enough for a start. You can save the world later.

1-5 A Warriors Job is to Kill

- Killing is your job. You don't have to like it, you just have to do it. When you are a civilian, you can choose what you want in your future.

- The act of killing is final. You can't change what you've done. If you are now a civilian, at least that much is over.

- Do not be ashamed to kill in war. If you didn't, you wouldn't be here right now.

- No training on earth could have prepared you for killing, so cut yourself some slack.

- How could you ever know what killing was like, unless you did it?

- You are suppose to feel. That's what makes you a good warrior, and not a murderer.

- You will always be a Warrior, so find other warriors, and get on with your life.

- Use your strength as a Warrior to guide you. Live by a code of Honor, and allow yourself to tolerate those who do not.

1-6 Hardening to Loss

- You can't be in war, and not feel loss. In fact, you can't live at all, and not feel loss at some time in your life.

- It's good to feel; that means you are capable of Love.

- Numbness is normal for a time. So give yourself some time to move out of it, if you are.

- You know the true meaning of "friendship"; use it wisely.

- The feeling of loss never completely goes away. It just gets easier to deal with.

- Grieving takes time. The waves get less and less each time they hit you.

- Find some kind of active release; a ride, a movie, a conversation with another vet. This helps keep your mind out of the re-wind mode.

- Get on with your life. Find something that makes you feel a little better, and do it.

- Be glad you're alive, with your whole life ahead of you.

1-7 Friendship and Survivor Guilt

- You know the true meaning of "friendship".

- You know what "trust" is.

- You know what "loss" is

- **Your friends thought you were worth dying for, Don't you think you're worth living for?**

- Remember your friends for the rest of your life: the good times, the hard times you shared.

- **Use the friendships of "trust" and "honor" as your standard, and your standard is excellence!**

1-8 Burn Out and Short Timer's Fear

- It is "normal" to feel burned out in a war.

- You may feel burned out with life. War does that too.

Just that simple.

- Give yourself some time, to feel like there's something of value to live for. It takes a while.

- There's nothing wrong with you if you don't give a shit about anything right now. It's the brain's way of surviving. You've just reached your limit. So cut yourself some slack!

- Listen up! You may not have come home. You may have just come back to the States. So don't sweat it! You Ain't Alone! We've got a plan for you.

- Feeling betrayed is normal. It sometimes goes with the turf of being a warrior. No one except another person with your experience will understand your Code of Honor. Don't expect them to.

- It may have been a culture shock and a life shock coming back to the States. But the States is about the same as you left it, **"You are Not!"**. Accept the fact that you have changed, and get on with your new life. It ain't so bad. In fact, it's damn right good!

Section Two: Home is Where Your Heart Was

2-1 Oh Shit! I'm Home!

One good thing about coming back from a war today, is that the American Public, for the most part, likes "our troops." Believe me, it makes it a hell of a lot easier at the airport, when people are smiling, clapping their hands, and waving Old Glory, rather than waving their middle fingers, and trying to hit you with a bag of dog shit or a rotten egg. And yet, regardless of how you're welcomed back, one thing remains as true today, and it did 40 years ago, "You're back!"

If you're fortunate (or unfortunate) to have family waiting for you, they've most likely planned a festive "Welcome Home" party just for you. Ah, it will be a wonderful event in your honor, that is until you find out that Momma-San has shit in your cake. You know, there's a hidden surprise waiting in the shadows?

Well then, after all the hugging and "Oh, how much we've worried about you" passes into a number of brewskies, or a few fingers of old Jack Daniels, you'll possibly start to think, "maybe I could just slink over to that corner for awhile." If you're like most of us Warriors, the conversations go downhill real fast. And after you field the usual brain-dead questions like "Did you kill anyone?" and "What was it like?" the back exit looks better and better all the time.

If you made it through the welcome home, I'm proud of you. If you didn't, I'm proud of you anyway. I made it up to the point when the hard liquor came out, and the "If I were runnin' that war" Nazis put on their arm bands, and the kids started "high steppin" around the table. Yep! Time for the Jar Head to make his bird! Dee-dee-mau! (Fly away, get the hell out!)

After any life threatening experience, a lot of folks try to find a little comfort in revisiting places that they enjoyed before the event. You know, kind of a feel good place in your head. Trouble is, **who you were is not who you are now.** so the places don't fit anymore, and that makes you uneasy. I'll give you an example.

I grew up in San Francisco, right in the city. So getting out to the country at times was a real nice change. Over the

Golden Gate Bridge, and heading north, was (and still is) a beautiful stretch of coast line along Mendocino County. It was a great place to relax and grab some good chow. You could have the "catch-of-the-day" anytime you felt like it. And a few of the quaint little restaurants were actually right at the end of the piers, where the fishing boats would dock. Don't know how it is now, but it was great back then.

Well anyway, it took me about one visit each to scratch all my so called friends off the list of "things to make me feel better." And there I was, joggin' in place like a dumb shit. Sort of like the saying, "all dressed up and no place to go."

I really needed some quiet time. Then all of a sudden, there it was! "My old stomping grounds along the Pacific Coast line," just popped into my green brain! "What a great place," I thought, as I immediately planned the trip. Trouble was, I didn't know that what actually came up in my old "Who I WAS" memory, was more like a "Bouncing Betty" (a land mine, that jumps up about a foot, and blows off your balls).

The thoughts of camping out sounded real good; guess I missed sleeping on the ground. So out came an old back pack, and I eagerly stuffed it with a few items for the trip. Not having a car on leave, I went down to the Greyhound Bus station, bought a ticket, and before I knew it, was on my way north for "rest and relaxation."

Rolling along the beautiful coastline did start to make me feel a little better, and except for the long-haired freak sitting next to me, the trip went pretty well. The bus stopped at a gas station next to a beautiful stand of redwood trees. I got out, and it truly was breath of fresh air. I'd about had it with the smell of sweat, incense, and dope from the dip-shits on the bus. And besides, they all looked like fashion models for "Losers-R-Us."

But there I stood, back in a beautiful place that held so many good memories of my past. And of course, it just didn't seem right to go into the "bush" without being suited up in Green Machine attire, so I ditty-bopped over to the station to change.

Stepping out of the bathroom appropriately dressed in jungle boots, utilities (green clothes) and back pack, all I needed was a rifle and a few grenades and I could have been ready for patrol. Although I instantly started getting real "unusual" stares from the local natives. It never crossed my mind, that this place, only a few years "in my past" hadn't really changed much at all. "I had changed," but didn't realize it at the time. That is, not quite yet. My wakeup call was about to go off like a thermite grenade (a powder that burns you to the bone).

You startin' to get the picture?

It was a beautiful California day, with blue skies and white, billowy clouds, creating a striking contrast to the green coastal mountains. I still recall how good it felt to be away from the family setting that had caused me so much disappointment, anger and resentment.

With my rucksack-styled backpack slung over one shoulder, I anxiously started out toward those beautiful, inviting mountains. Blending in with the colors and rhythms of nature was (and still is) how I felt most comfortable in the "bush."

I crossed over a paved road, through a weathered and broken split-rail fence, then headed out across a beautiful level field. The sweet, fragrant smell of alfalfa and wild flowers, combined with the salt spray of the sea, filled the air.

About half way across the field, I noticed a young, very attractive woman and her child, just entering the same path I had taken, and heading in my direction. They were dressed in the usual new-age, hippie fashion of the times, which didn't seem out of the ordinary, so it didn't set off any alarms in my brain-housing-group.

My sense of purpose and worth were rekindled for a moment. "Freedom for this small and happy little girl is why I was fighting," I thought, and "Everything will be OK now." At that moment, believed I had finally made it home. But that's when it happened!

Not more than 10 meters away from me, the woman suddenly veered off the trail. Grabbing her child by the arm, the little girl's head was jerked back, as the woman violently pulled her daughter behind her paisley skirt.

Quickly, the child peeked back around her mother's

leg. And what had just been a cute, warm little smile, instantly changed to a frightened, confused and wide-eyed expression as she looked at "me!"

"What the hell's going on here?" I thought. "I used to come here all the time before I joined the Corps."

The tension mounted, as I began to pass the two, keeping alert to any sudden movement in my direction, just in case the woman had a weapon. Overly defensive perhaps, but my experience "in-country" had taught me that a man, woman or child could kill you with equal ease.

Not daring any lengthy eye contact, but principally maintaining peripheral surveillance of their actions, I managed to get about 30 feet past the two. Man, the adrenalin was really pumpin' by that time, and I could see the anger in this woman's eyes when I did quickly glance her way. And just when I thought I was in the clear, the bomb went off!

The mother violently lunged toward me! I snapped around and met her gaze. In an instant, I was back in the jungle and ready to kill again, didn't matter who or what. But as I waited for "contact," I was watching in disbelief, because what I thought was just an unfriendly glare, was transformed into "absolute" hate and rage.

I took a step toward her, but was stopped dead in my tracks, as she yelled at the top or her lungs,

"You fucking, Baby Killing PIG!"

And in less than a heartbeat, the already panicked little girl, began to cry hysterically.

To see those beautiful, big blue eyes, filled with such dread and fear of me, then to watch the tears roll down those rosy little cheeks, broke my heart. Just a few weeks before that, blood soaked and in agony over what I had done, I had carried another little girl to the chopper pad.

Of course I was now in a rage myself, **but at myself!** "Maybe this hippie bitch is right?" I thought, and for a moment, I just stood there.

Looking down at my clothing, I felt naked and

ashamed. "I guess I really don't belong here anymore" kept rolling through my mind. But I wondered "where" did I belong?

Traumatized and alone, I wandered up into the hills to spend the night. And the next morning, adding insult to injury, I headed back to the bus stop with a full blown case of Poison Oak. No shit! Remember me telling you "never" to say "can things get any worse?"

The bus ride back to San Francisco was a little better, because no one wanted to sit next to me. Guess they thought that surely I must have either fleas or lice, as I scratched my way back to the city.

Watching the coastline roll by again, even in my thick green skull, I could see that things had drastically change in my life. I was no longer the person I was, and didn't have a clue as to what to do about it.

The next day was the "straw that broke the camel's back." Against my better judgment, and with the insistent promptings of my so called friends, I attended a high school dance. Remember, I was still only 19 years old. Well, to make a long story short, after my old football coach called me an asshole (must have a bad practice that day) and after starting a major fight in the bathroom (I was feeling a little aggressive), I decided to get drunk that night, grab a bottle of calamine lotion and head back to base the next day.

"Things were sure as hell not the same in civilian life; maybe it would be better on the base?" I thought. And, after my "wake up call" with the Peace Loving Goddess of Hate and Rage, I now realized that I had **changed a lot**. But I still couldn't figured out where all that "free love" was. It sure wasn't headin' my way, that was for sure. And since in those days, us Warriors called the peace sign the footprint of the American Chicken, I was goin' back to where I knew at least I was armed, and surrounded by crazy people like myself. Peace signs were in the dress code.

So what's the point of all this you ask? Real simple. When you arrive at the airport, or at "Mommy" or "Daddy's" house, that cute little sucker, who used to mine for nose gold, ain't the one showin' up at the front door.

You are **not** the person you were when you left!

Don't be a dumb ass like the Old Sarge was. And just what does all that mean? It means you now need to find out who this **new** person on the block really is, and plan out his or her new life. Don't worry, I've got a few tactics for all that. Rest assured, I'm not letting you Warriors cross that field like I did, without some serious firepower to cover your asses.

Now, you'll need some body armor for the next few topics, but **keep your safeties on**, this may(?) be friendly fire................... Let's move it out!

2-2 Hi Honey, Who are You?

The "welcome home party" is over, everyone's sobered up, you're back home, and you're finally able to spend some quality time with your partner. Trouble is, the conversation is going nowhere. Nothing really seems to be that important, so you wing it. You know, make believe you're interested in little Jimmy's soccer game, Aunt Sophie's broken hip, or little Susie's ballet performance. There's lots of important catchin' up to do. You understand that every spouse does this from time to time, but this time, you're about to jump out of the second story window, and take your chances on a well executed PLF (Parachute Landing Fall).

About the time you're able to gracefully weasel out of the house to "fetch" some milk (and beer) from the local store, you realize, "Man! I'm in deep shit now!", and you should. Not only are you dealing with the nightmare list we've talked about so far, you've also got to fit in all the normal stress of a family and a relationship. That is, a relationship with someone who doesn't have a clue about how you're actually feeling. It also doesn't make you feel warm and tingly when you notice that your partner is carrying around the phone with their finger poised over the speed dial to call 911.

Somehow, your war stories aren't having the effect you'd like. You're not getting a "Oh, come over for a big huggy" reaction. In fact, you're getting just the opposite. Now it's a few steps back while your partner's saying "OK kids, go over to the neighbor's house and play, Mommy and Daddy need to talk. And here, put the keys to the car in your pocket for Mommy."

"So what do I do?", you ask. Well, first of all, with three ex-wives, I'm not a marriage counselor, but I have seen it work out both ways. If the Veteran goes out and immediately gets some help with his or her problems, and if the partner can tough it out during the period it takes to get through it all, there **is** a chance. This depends on how much you love one another, how much patience you have and how much progress is made quickly. But most importantly, it depends on whether or not the partner even likes this "new person" in their life. This can be a very difficult situation, especially if children are involved.

If you, the Warrior, will not admit you have some problems, like I didn't, then your relationship is pretty much down the shit tube, plain and simple. I completely denied the truth during my first marriage, until one night my wife (at the time) thought she'd surprise me.

I was tired and pissed off (as usual) from working all day at a job that I hated, it was late, and I was standing by the closet in our bedroom, in the dark. Reaching into the closet for a change of clothes, my back was turned toward the door and the hallway, also dark. There were carpets on the floors of the little apartment we'd rented, so walking around barefoot didn't make a lot of noise.

My wife knew that even though I wouldn't talk about it anymore, I was definitely dealing with issues from the war. It was obvious from the cold sweats and my waking up screaming from the recent barrage of nightmares. Don't ask me why, but she decided she was gonna' play G.I. Jane that night, and try to see how close she could sneak up on me before I noticed. A real bad choice.

For a moment, I had let my guard down. I was not "aware of my surroundings at all times." Guess I thought it was a little safe in my own home? But slowing, in the shadows of the carpet jungle, the Viet Cong approached my position. Finally feeling her eyes, at about four feet away, I "flashed" back to the war! It was kill or be killed!

But I had no weapon! "I'd have to use my hands" I thought, and "Go for the throat!", instantly flashed through my brain.

You don't really think at times like that, you react, and that's just what I did. Spinning around, I grabbed her by the throat and pinned her to the wall, as she desperately gasped for air. But something was wrong! "This is not the war!" finally fired in my head.

All she could do was to keep gasping and whispering, "Don't kill me, please don't kill me!"

Realizing what I had just done, I let go, stepped back, and "assumed the position" as "Asshole of the Year." She turned on the light, looked at me, took a sigh, then dropped her head while holding her throat, and left the room.

The next day, her mother called. And asking my wife,

"How's Andy doing?" she replied, "Oh, he's ok, he just almost killed me last night."

From that moment on, I figured our relationship had about the life span of a water buffalo in a napalm strike. Interesting thing was, we did love each other, and parted the best of friends. I couldn't blame her. Damn, I didn't want to live with me either.

This whole situation was **NOT** my wife's fault. It was MY fault, for denying I had a problem. She just wanted to kid around a little bit, and I almost turned it into a little killing.

Do you get my point yet? If you love your companion, don't deny your problems!

Now, let's get back to the "What do I do?" question. The first step, is to read this book all the way to the end. "You don't have to like it, you just have to do it." Besides, the last section may give you a laugh or two. Then after reading the book, you'll need to be honest with yourself, and have a heart to heart talk with your partner.

If you both decide that the relationship is worth the effort, and you love each other enough to give it that 100% effort, then you'll need to get to a VA counselor ASAP. And by the way, don't say "Oh, I'll try." When people whine about trying, that means, they've quit before they even got started. "Don't try, just do!" Same thing with "I'll do my best." Bull shit! I want a 100% effort, or nothing. And if you do drop out, you'd better be pukin!

If you can't find a VA counselor, and your last resort is a civilian shrinker, then make sure that person has combat experience. Why? That's easy. It's because if the psychiatrist or psychologist you hook up with is not a Combat Vet, then they won't have any more of an idea what's goin' on in your head than the partner sitting next to you. And guess who ends up lookin' like the asshole, and feeling even more guilt they don't need? Yep! That's an affirmative, it's the Warrior. "That be me."

I've learned long ago, that "professional help only helps if it's professional." That is, coming from a base of common experience. But sometimes, no matter how hard you work at it, loving each other isn't enough to live with each other.

That's another one of those custom fit situations. It depends on two people sharing a common goal: their own individual happiness, and the happiness of the family. Not to mention a bright future that's both stable and nurturing for the children.

The only thing I want to remind you Young Warriors of, is that no matter how "any" relationship works out, keep your focus on "Honor" all the way through it. You didn't ask to be this new person; it's just what happened when you went to war. It's unfortunate and damn difficult for the person you left behind, who still loves the person you were. And it's unfortunate and extremely difficult for you, living as the person you've now become.

Be advised, **it's nobody's fault**. And if you "are" able to work it out, that's wonderful. If you can't work it out, then at least part best of friends. I think that's the least you can do for the person you still love. If I did it, as brain-fried as I was, then you sure as hell can too! And once again (until you puke?) "You are not alone!"

Keep that body armor on, and pass a vest over to your partner and/or spouse. This next topic is gonna sting a bit.

Now, let's break camp and Move Out! The sooner you get done with this sweep, the better you'll be.

2-3 Spouses/Partners; Jealousy and Anger

As the wars in Afghanistan and Iraq labor on, troop rotation has become a way of life for our men and women fighting overseas. However, one major difference now is that many more women are in the ranks than back in my time. Another difference is that large units of troops are deployed at the same time. But just how they're sent overseas actually makes little or no difference, because the results of war are the same. And both the Warriors and their loved ones are dealing with the results.

We need to talk over a few things here, for the sake of the wives, husbands, partners and friends left behind. Because it's very difficult for you as well, waiting for the "bad" news, and worrying every day about what's going on. And then wondering **who the hell just came through your front door** when it's all over.

Your warrior looks about the same, their eyes may be a little darker, perhaps more sunken into the sockets, they're a bit jumpy now, and can't seem to relax, but generally, you can't see any "major" difference.

You might expect a little of that, but you're having a hard time imagining what they've actually gone though. The most important thing on your mind is, "They're finally home". The fact is my friends, these warriors have just experienced things that you will never understand. That is, unless you've lived through a "life and death" experience like theirs or your own.

Now, one thing needs to be said right up front. Upon returning home, your Warrior doesn't love you any less. In fact, they love you even more. Life has now become a precious commodity to each of them. Maybe you've noticed how protective they've become, to insure your safety? And if they've had to kill children, then your children's safety goes beyond words.

One of the problems that seems to be coming up in the current wars is that of "misunderstood intent." I'll explain that as clearly as I can. If you've read this "Warrior's Guide" up to this point, you may begin to see patterns of behavior that you recognize in your Veteran. They are needing to process the feelings of their experiences all the time. They need a release from the pressure and pain that we'll discuss a bit later on. And if they can't find an outlet to release this pain peacefully, it then turns to anger and rage.

Unfortunately, when this kind of emotion is released in that manner, consciously or unconsciously, the closest person around usually gets the worst of it.

Please don't feel guilty if they don't seem to be able to talk about the war with you. They know you won't really understand, and they love you far too much to drag you into their nightmare. It has nothing to do with you. It has everything to do with them, trying to keep from exploding and letting you down. Remember, they think that you think they are your special hero. Heroes must be "strong" and not hurt anyone they love or feel is of great value. There will be a lot of times when they first come back that you'll just need to give them some space, to space out.

OK, here we go with the touchy part. If they find other Combat Vets to talk with, and I strongly suggest they do, some of those Veterans may be of the opposite sex. But don't sweat it. It's not their intent, to go off and cheat on you, they just need to process their experiences with others that completely understand; doesn't matter if it's a man or a woman. That's gonna' be a hard one to deal with, but deal with it you must.

If you had a good relationship before they went to war, you'll have a good relationship now. That is, if you both work at it together. Fact is, I've never seen a relationship you didn't have to work at. So I guess you could say if you don't work at it, it won't work out. Damn! I'm startin' to sound like one of them silk-slipper poets. You know, the ones that shuffle around the apartment, talkin' to their poodles. Well, the fact is, I'm sure as shit not wearin' slippers, and you ain't little ToTo, so then, shall we continue?

One of the interesting things to me is that many of the Vets I know, including myself, felt that they would do anything to keep their family and relationship together. If it didn't work out, it usually wasn't the Vet's choice, it just got to be too much for the spouse.

I've talked to a number of woman over the years who **were** married to combat veterans. It seems to be the same scenario. The wives became frustrated listening to the same old stories, over and over, while seeing the one they loved, not only suffering, but never getting any better. They felt helpless.

And just like everyone else, spouses have their breaking point too. They need to survive. Hell, they need to do more than just survive, they need to get on with their own lives, and find some real joy in it. That is not an easy thing to do with someone who is always pissed off, hates everything, and can't seem to get his ass out of the Twilight Zone. What do you expect will happen, living with a loser like that?

If you are the Warrior in this kind of situation, and you **are not** showing any signs of progress (of dealing with your baggage) then you may as well pack your baggage, and head for the exit sign. Even in a new "still in the honeymoon" relationship, you are still gonna need to be working on gettin' your shit together. If your new partner comes home one day, only to find you sitting in the easy chair (drunk?) with a glazed-over, blank look in your eyes, dry-firing your weapon at the TV screen, it's a fair guess you ain't gonna have a partner for very long. In fact the honeymoon has just ended, and you've just screwed the pooch (see Glossary).

Once again, it isn't easy for either the spouse, or the Veteran. And it sure as hell is not the **fault** of either the Spouse or the Veteran if things don't work out in the long run. After talking with many Warriors over the years, and to many ex-wives of Warriors as well, I can't help but feel a sadness, that so many truly fine people had to suffer so much.

As to the wives and partners caught in this backlash of Afghanistan and Iraq, I can only say this: your returning warrior is simply **not the same person** that you hugged and kissed at the airport on their way to war. And it's up to both of you to fight the next battle together. If you think about it, the longer you stay together now, and walk the same path, the more common ground you'll share with this new person. And the more common ground you share, the more likely it will be that you'll share the same future.

As to my fellow Warriors, the choice is up to you, to work at getting a handle on your emotions, your problems, and make a new life for yourself. Or you can become a brain-fried shit-bird, like I was, and waste 30 years in figuring it all out. If you want a relationship to continue with your family, then you've got to work at it as if it's the only goal in your life, because everyone's future is at stake here.

You know you **can** do it. The real question is, do you want to? And in the state of mind you may be in right now, you may not even know that you do. Just remember, no matter what you've been through, or are about to go through, us Old Warriors have been there to "break trail."

Now, hang in there, we've got a few more shitters to burn.

2-4 An Old Warrior's Esteemed View on Women

At my station in life, being what some would call "long in the tooth," in other words, an "old fart," it may help some of you young warriors to consider what this Old Leather Neck has learned along the way, in this forced march we call life. Don't worry, I'll keep it brief. We've gotta' get back in the saddle, and keep cleanin' the cobwebs out of your skull, but I thought you'd enjoy taken a break about now.

What have I learned about women? You ask. Well, that ain't real simple, because women aren't real simple to figure out. They sure as hell didn't sleep through their training films on men. I'll bet you male warriors kinda' wish you could say the same, don't ya?

If I may speak personally for a bit, the first thing I like to say, is that I love women. (There he goes, kissin' ass already!) You say! Well maybe, but at my age, I damn well know who's ass I wanta' kiss and who's ass I wanta' kick. So anyway, zip it up, and listen up!

As I was saying, I love women (What? No smart ass comment?) I love "everything" about'em, and I ain't no shit-for- brains pervert standing over in the shadows with my zipper down. I just think they're wonderful.

You'll have to remember, that I grew up in a time when gas was 25 cents a gallon, and women used to glide when they walked; some still do (you know, they didn't bounce up and down like they have an itch they can't scratch?).

Being old fashioned, I truly appreciate beautiful, long, flowing hair, good manners at chow time, and a bayonet-sharp tongue that can bring a man to his knees in one cutting sentence. That's right! A woman with spunk (that's not a smelly woman for you Marines, it means frisky). You know the type. It's the woman that's got the "I'm not taken any shit from any man, no matter how big the son of a bitch is!" attitude. It's the "if I can't kick his ass, I'll sew his ass in a sheet when he's drunk, and beat the shit out of this maggot" attitude.

Now for you women that may have decided to read this book (against your partners wishes ? Ya see, that's spunk!), I would like to make the following comment about men.

Ladies, as I see it, the first major handicap men have, is that when they're younger (and some never change), they are guided by, and think with, two brains. That's right. There's one in that cube of gray shit above their shoulders, and that little "twitchy" one, hangin' between their legs. And I can tell you for a fact, that little one does get in the way of clear thinking most of the time.

The really interesting thing is, that even though women are not men, they have mastered an understanding of the "little brain" very well, and know how to control its thoughts to their advantage. It's not our fault ladies, it's just that men aren't that complicated, and when we're young, we've got a real problem in deciding which brain to use. Unfortunately, the twitchy one takes over most of the time.

The second, and almost as bad as the "duel of the brains," is the problem of the male ego (no Marines, it's not that yellow, slimy shit that looks like eggs). Many combat vets that I've known, including yours truly, don't have much, if any of the usual asshole ego. We've been battle tested; not much to prove after that. But a lot of men still hold on to the "I'm stronger "I'm in charge," "I can piss up a tree farther" macho (not corn chips, Jar Heads) attitude. And to be real honest with you ladies, most men are fairly insecure with their manhood anyway, and the whole act they're putting on is mostly bullshit.

You know what I mean don't you? When men are acting like "they give the orders around here!", all you've gotta' do, is cuddle-up a bit, maybe swing your shapely hips, and you've usually got'em. If that doesn't do it, with a sexy wink, and a glance to the bedroom, POW! The little brain has taken over completely. You ladies are now in full control of the steering column and even if your destination has changed from the other room to the market to pick up groceries, the little brain is hopeful and obedient. It's not that men don't make good decisions, hell, a broken watch is right twice a day. I must admit, that I can't even guess at the times I've said (secretly), "Damn, why didn't I listen to her!"

Now, another thing you gals really do need to understand is that besides a paper-thin, delicate ego, and the need to prove self-worth, men really feel a strong need to "provide" for their loved ones. I'm not one of those eggheads that digs through the shitters of old villages, to figure out if papa-san liked boys more than girls, but I do know, that this drive to provide makes men feel really good when there's enough chow on the table. And if they do an exceptional job of it, they might even get lucky that night? (The little brain?)

It is my humble judgment, that the biggest mistake a woman can make, is giving her power away to a man. For you Devil Dogs out there, that means, letting a shit-for-brains take over the mission, when you damn well know you can do a better job of it yourself. I'm sure that there are many woman, who like men, have said (not silently) "Damn it! Why in the hell did I listen to that moron?"

If a man is mature, confident, and knowledgeable (in the subject being talked about), he will listen, evaluate and discuss decisions peacefully. Especially, if you are wearing something appealing to the all-seeing, "twitchy" observer. However, sometimes things are not peaceful, and the man ends the conversation by stomping his feet, and pounding his chest like a shit throwing baboon!

Why am I saying all this? You ask. Real simple. It's because I have been a shit throwing baboon, pulled the pin on three marriages, and regretfully, caused some very beautiful women a lot of grief.

Many of us old combat vets thought that if we poured out guts out about our war experiences, and threw enough shit in the fan, our companions would get the point. But the only thing that really happened from all of our "communicating" this way, was that **we** got the point; that is, the point of a black pen, pressing down on the divorce papers, while some slithery, scum-bag attorney counted our money on the way to his bank.

I've met a good many divorced women over the course of my somewhat checkered life, and a fair number of them were the ex-wives of veterans. So I really do know that maturity, confidence and knowledge doesn't always end up in the same package. It's just the ideal. (Found one yet?)

I also know, full well, that sometimes a situation can turn ugly. And on this, I cannot speak for every veteran, only myself, and those I associate with. Except for an accident, like the one I spoke of with my first wife, neither I, nor any of the combat vets I have known, have ever hit a woman. To hit a woman is an act of cowardice in my book. Sure, I've blocked a couple of good ones coming in my direction, which I deserved, but never struck back.

This is a demonstration of a man's desire to dominate, and control, to take every bit of self-esteem from a woman, and make feel no more than a slave to his every wish. Hell, an asshole like this, may as well hand his wife a burlap bag and send her out in the fields.

Every "Honorable" Warrior that I know, feels like what I'm about to say. And it may offend a few, but "I don't give a shit."

This is what "I" would like to see happen! Be glad to help out too! Let's see if we can keep them in order.

On behalf of all women and children:

Any man who beats his wife (on his first offense) should be flogged in public, and then beaten to within an inch of his life; the second offense is death. Any man who rapes a woman should be immediately castrated, the death sentence then to be decided upon by the victim. Any son of a bitch that rapes or molests a child should be killed without mercy. Real simple isn't it? I can already hear the Marines on the ready-line, forming up to volunteer.

Oh, so you think I'm a bit radical do you? Try talking to some of my police friends, or children's services. They'll snap your asshole shut in about 3 seconds. If this warrior approach doesn't deter new future offenders, it will at least take care of the scum on the streets as we speak, and give a little closure, maybe even a sense of real justice to the victims. I find more of value in the cat box every morning, than in these worthless, child abusing scum.

Out here in New Mexico, we have a lot of old, abandoned, vertical mine shafts. One round to the head and a bag of lime tied to his chest (keeps down the flies) would save tax payers a whole bunch of money, and get rid of repeat offenders. There's plenty of room for **everyone** out here, including the maggot clergy hiding behind their next victims. Guess I'll have to send a copy of this book to the Vatican. Well then, that about raps up my stand for Women and Children's rights. Suppose I can put my K-bar down now and get on with our somewhat lighter topic.

Woman can be beautiful, loving human beings: thoughtful, sensitive and caring. It's their nature to express the emotions that help children grow up in the same way. Woman can also be cold, calculating, and as vicious as a junk yard dog. To me that's what makes them so great! Us men are never quite sure if we're gonna' reach in the duffle bag and pull out a soft little kitten, or a copperhead. Women are mysterious beings who keep men guessing all of the time.

No matter how long a man knows a woman, he's never really sure what she's thinking. Kind of keeps things interesting. How many times have you men asked yourself, "What the hell did she mean?" or "What the hell is she really thinking?" Interesting isn't it?

Now, for you ladies, here's a real "positive" thing about men. We're not all assholes! Yep! It's true. This is why when a Warrior gets his act together, that is, works out his problems to the point where he can become an asset (not asshole) in society, he's really nice to be around. You still may not care to live with him, but he's great to take for walks (just kiddin').

At this stage in his psychological (big word, means emotional) growth, he's not trying to prove himself to anyone, let alone the men's-macho-show-your-ass-club. He's not asking you to pull his finger, and he doesn't belch in front of your friends, demonstrating some new form of human speech. He's thoughtful, because he appreciates every single thing around him: from a hot shower, to a beautiful sunrise, and good conversation, or a cold beer on a hot day. He counts his blessings, because he's alive to do so. And ladies, if you can "find" one of these Combat Vets you just happen to love, he will love you unconditionally, and die to protect you. Not too bad is it?

So you see, my Brothers, just how it can be for you. "Get your shit together" is your most important goal. Make your life a reflection of who you've now become, and who you have become enjoys the hell out of life. All of a sudden you can go from a shitbird reject in society, to a rare and highly prized individual who is a real joy to be around. It's sort of like a rebirth; you know, kinda like that buzzard comin' up out of the ashes in that 55 gallon drum when you burn the shitters? Same-e-same.

Oh, and one last comment to you ladies. If by some stroke of twisted fate, you happen to hook up with a Marine, you're gonna' have to be easy on him. For example, I hope you don't mind the way I write; it doesn't come that quick.

Being a Marine, I've gotta' start out with "Big" colored pens (you know, the marks-a-lot kind) then work my way down to a pencil. Us Marines like to keep things "real" simple. Takes a while to get down to fine tuned, and complicated tools. It's like if I said to "put on your thinkin' caps," instantly a Marine reaches for his kevlar helmet and grabs his rifle for security; chambering a round helps even more. Anyway, we're a good bunch, it's just that most of us grunts aren't quite center of bubble. But we damn sure get the job done, don't we?

Alright then, the Smoking Lamp is Out! That means the cigarette break is over, time to get back at it.

You might want'a grab an extra magazine of ammo for the next topic.

If we flush out the "Boogie-Man" on this one, we don't want to run short; that is, before we pop him a new asshole in the middle of his head!

2-5 The Pain Inside

By the time you've started to figure out that you're now at least one can shy of a six pack, and you feel like you're about to have what the yuppies call a panic attack (every waking minute), you're at a critical point, and you damn well know it. When those emotional "flood gates" open up, your senses are on full alert, your chest feels like Hulk Hogan's got you in a bear hug, and you know that any second you're gonna puke all over your mother-in-law's new carpet. There's also no doubt you've just gained a full hat size on your throbbing head. Yep, you're definitely on your way down the old shit tube, headin' for Fly Paradise. Been there, and didn't have a clue why, but you do. So let's quit lolly-gaggin' around, and figure out how you can avoid putting yourself through any more grief than necessary.

First off, nothing is gonna completely stop the pain you're feeling. Why? Because you haven't done anything to get rid of it yet. It's like having a real nice sliver of wood jammed under your fingernail. Unless you get the sucker out, it's sure as hell gonna keep causing you a lot of pain. "So how do you get the sliver out?" you ask. Well my friends, this ain't launchin' the Space Shuttle. You know, rocket science? It's just a matter of a few simple steps, and you'll start to feel a whole lot better.

Remember our conversation on "loss?" Well, all emotions kind of follow the same Kahuna (Hawaiian Sea God) rule. That is, all emotions come in sets of waves, just like the ocean. Some waves are closer together, and some farther apart. That depends on what emotion, how intensely you're feeling it, and how you're brain-housing-group is set up to handle it. In other words, everybody deals with emotions a little differently. But one thing always remains the same. If you don't find a way to "turtle" under the waves, you're definitely gonna' wipe out and get your ass kicked in the process.

OK, so now you're ready to listen to the Old Sarge? You're in a "world of hurt," and you want to know how they get the sliver out, and start "turtling" under the waves? Well, my smooth-shelled friends, you do that by opening up a dialogue (Marines: not a dead tree in the forest). What this means, is that you get your ass down to the Veteran's Outreach Center, and start talking about the whole damn mess in your head. Getting with other Combat Vets will certainly help too, but you need professional help. And if you need a quick "med" or two to get through a few sets of waves, so be it.

There's no shame in relying on the legal drug cartel for a little while. You just don't wanta' take the Zombie meds for the rest of your life. And, you **will not** have to, so don't sweat it. Just remember, "live one day at a time," get through each day, and don't worry about tomorrow just yet. Maybe it will help you to think of it like being on the rifle range.

You've got the correct windage and elevation all zeroed in, you breathe out, and gently pull the trigger. At that moment, you are completely focused through the rear sight, at the target, you can feel when it's a perfect shot. Same-e-Same. For the moment, you'll need to focus on an emotional target, to "cap" the one that's causing you the most grief. It could be any one of a number of feelings, and when we go back over the list in Section Five, maybe you can figure out which one to talk over first.

I'm gonna say this again. If you've been through a war, and you're feeling emotions that are controlling your life in a bad way, don't try to ignore, or deny that there **is a problem you need to work on.** I suppressed my feelings and denied my actions for over 13 years. When I finally did break down, and eventually, most people do, the "built up" emotions almost killed me. You do not want that happening to you, and there is no reason why it should. The trouble is, you never really know how much stress you can stand, or when the flood gates are gonna open and sweep you down shit river. I'll give you an example.

I was traveling through Denver, Colorado, on my way back to Phoenix. Having just driven from Mississippi, I was in need of a brain-break and some chow. So after bolting down a delicious, artery clogging meal at the Land of the Golden Crotches, I decided to take in a movie. I never cared much for driving in those days, because it gave me too much time to think about things I was trying to "forget." Trouble was, I didn't have some Old Sarge tellin' me **"You don't forget about it, Dip-Shit, your sorry ass learns how to**

deal with it!"

Anyway, not having the resource of this great philosopher riding shotgun with me, I had no clue of what was about to happen. All I remember is that for some reason beyond my understanding, memories of the war were dominating my thoughts.

Pulling up to the movie theaters, all housed in one building, I checked out the selection. There were several choices that didn't set off any bells and whistles for me, but the one with Sylvester Stallone sounded real inviting. I always liked Stallone, so without thinking much about it, I walked up, bought a ticket, and walked in, just like a fly buzzin' into the web. The movie was "Rambo, First Blood."

As the story unfolded, I found myself saying, "Oh, that's OK, I just about swam in Agent Orange," and "Oh, that's OK, I've been through that kind of training," and so on. By the time he was surrounded in the Sheriff's Office, I had identified with every one of his feelings and every bit of his insanity. But for some reason I just could "not get up" and leave the theater. I had to see it to the end. What I didn't realize, was that the end of this movie was the end of my life as I had known it.

When Rambo "broke down," I "broke down." And as he described being unable to find the body parts of his brother, my own flash-back-nightmare was in full swing. Gripping the armchair with all my strength, while tears ran down my face, I was frozen and afraid to move a muscle. As the floodgates opened after years of denial, I was caught in a fast-foreword replay of every single event I had tried to forget about, every killing, every brother lost, every traumatic event of the war rolled through my brain like a freight train. The movie ended, all the people got up and left, and there I sat, tears still rolling down my face. Finally the manager came over and asked me if I was alright. Feeling on the verge of "losing control," I forced myself up, and as I passed him, said "Hell of a movie."

There just happened to be a bar a short walk from the theater, and as I headed in that direction, I just kept repeating " I AM a Marine, I AM a Marine." At that moment the realization hit me, that I had only one person in the world I could tell about this. I had no support base at all! After several beers and a shot or two, I started to feel calm enough to make a phone call. My only friend suggested I get to a professional as quickly as possible, and I agreed. My emotions were out of control, and I knew it.

This is NOT what you want happening to "you." I truly don't know how I made it through all the shit of that moment with only a few drinks and a single phone call. And sometimes, when this same thing happened to other Vets, they "didn't" make it.

So then, you can either take it the "Hard-but-controlled" way, or you can take it the "Harder-down-the-shit-tube" way. Neither way is easy, but you can certainly get your life in order, with a "controlled program" of professional guidance. With an attitude of denial, you can ruin what life you have, until you go over the edge of the dam, or through the flood gates like I did. Both are a nightmare.

There is one other, not so pleasant, possibility that you might consider as to living with the effects of traumatic stress, and it's kind of a subtle thing. There are a very "few" individuals that seem to be able to push their emotions to a place in their mind, that allows them to appear to be acting like most other people. You know, whatever the hell normal is.

I've known only two Veterans like this, and it was very uncomfortable to be around either of them. Having been through all the same problems, it was obvious to me, they were both Dink-ki-dow (misspelled, but means "crazy" in Vietnamese). These men may have been able to hold off exploding just yet, but the stress of their experiences did in fact have a major effect on their lives. They were extremely insecure, would get violently angry, and had about the lowest self-esteem I'd ever seen. They have lasted this way for over 30 years! And Brothers and Sisters, this ain't the way to go!

These men never wanted to face their problems head on, deal with'em, and get onto a new and better life. I will not bullshit you. It's not easy to go through the process, but it is a hell of a lot better than living a lie; "pretending" to be "normal". Far better in my way of thinkin' to be proud of yourself, to feel good about the life you've decided on, and to be happy living it.

Many of you Young Warriors are feeling exactly like I did when I came back from war. That's one thing that doesn't change with time, and you have basically two choices. Go with the new help now available to you, or go with the way I dealt with it until I almost killed myself.

You'll have to remember, back in the 60's, we Vets didn't have any help. We had no choice like you Young Veterans of today's wars. But one thing was certain. In the state of mind I was in at the time, I was definitely a threat to everyone around me.

Surprisingly, when "I" went "dink-ki-dow", I did have enough sense to know that if I had taken some of the illegal drugs of the time, I would have most likely ended up on some nice tall building, shooting the Viet Cong in the streets of San Francisco. "So what did I do?" you ask.

Remembering my Drill Instructors patient and gentle words, "Pain is good! Now, you shit eatin' maggots, drop down and feel the goodness!" I decided to run until I dropped. I've always felt honored to be a Marine, and the Corps, once again, saved my simple ass in those days of real pain.

"Feeling the goodness" went on for days. I'd run until my legs gave out, then do push-ups until couldn't stand. Once on my feet again, I'd shuffle until I could run, repeating the process until I couldn't get up. This continued until the pain in my body exceeded the pain in my head. Then, after each treatment of love and kindness to my scraped and bruised body, I'd go back to my apartment, and drink until I passed out. This is NOT the way to get through the waves of emotion! And I don't want to hear about any of you youngins taken that road. You don't need to, in these days of caring, professional help. I just didn't know what else to do at the time, and "surrender is not in my creed."

If you don't let the emotions build up, you will pass these sets of waves very quickly. For example, when I accidentally discovered the Veteran's Outreach Center, I started going to a VA counselor twice a week, and the group meetings twice a week. No bullshit, as bad as I was at the time, I was still ashamed to admit that I had a problem. I was actually "embarrassed" to walk into the Center the first time, so I understand how you might feel about that.

Here's the good news. As brain-fried as I was, once I started talking about the worse problems first (for me, survivor guilt, and killing kids) I never went through those intense waves again. I slowed way down on the drinking, and knew that if I really needed some legal meds, they were always available. I tried them a couple of times just for the hell of it.

Once I got into the system, it really felt good to know that other Vets felt just like me, and that someone really gave a shit about our well being. It was sorta' like being part of a family, and I hadn't felt that since I left the Corps.

There's just one more thing I'd like to say before moving to our next section. You Marines and Spec. Ops. Warriors, listen up especially.

I truly understand, that most Warriors have a hard time with weakness in others. But admitting how you're feeling about some of these topics, doesn't make you weak, it makes you smart. That's because if you deal with some of these issues now, it can help you to do your job a whole lot better, and it'll be a whole lot safer for your fellow Warriors next time you go into combat. Nobody wants to go into a battle with people they can't trust. That's not what honor and friendship are all about. If you're feeling burned out to the point that its affecting your job, chances are real good you **are not alone**.

I'm "respectfully" suggesting that you think about this real hard, and don't put your life or the lives of your team in more danger. You've already got enough to deal with. That's all I feel at liberty to say about this. You'll have to figure it out on your own, and decide for yourself.

But be advised, that whether you believe in "why" you are (or were) fighting in these wars, the fact remains that it is (or was) your duty to do so. You are carrying on a tradition that only Warriors can understand, and "together", we "Will overcome ANY obstacle". You will never be alone in these times.

I am honored to be within this Brother/Sisterhood. And know this: each of your lives is as precious to me as my own, and the memories of the beloved "friends" we have all lost. Keep the faith, and remember, "And this too, shall pass."

Let's move along to the next Section, and another war

you'll have to fight. At least in this one, you'll have a say on tactics. You may not like the battleground, but if you hold fast under fire, the results can be a life well worth the effort, a life you'll truly enjoy living, with honor as your guide.

Now, keep your head down, and let's "Move Out!"

Section Two Summary

2-1 Oh Shit! I'm Home

- The American public "now" likes the Military.

- You're back, and like it or not, you ain't the same person that left.

- Get through the "welcome homes" and all the disappointments, then get on with your new life.

- Friends and family may not be the same toward you.

- Find new friends to talk with about your feelings; others with similar experiences.

- You "will" make it through the transition; you'll have to choose how soon.

2-2 Hi Honey, Who Are You?

- Adapting the new you to family life can be very difficult.

- You'll have to carry all of your war baggage, and the family stress of raising a family as well.

- You'll have to decide if it's possible to live in a family.

- Get some professional help, as long as its someone with similar experiences.

- Sometimes loving each other isn't enough to live with each other.

- Stay honorable in your actions.

- You are not who you were. It may be difficult for your spouse or partner to love who you have now become.

- It's no one's fault. You are just human. War does this to people.

2-3 Spouses/Partners: Jealousy and Anger

- It was very difficult for you as a spouse and/or partner waiting for the "death notice."

- It was also very difficult for you as a spouse and/or partner to deal with how your warrior had changed so much.

- Your Warrior has had experience that you cannot possibly understand. So cut yourself some slack.

- Your Warrior Loves you more than ever, and wants to protect you more than ever.

- Your Veteran needs time to "process" his or her experiences, "space to space out."

- Veterans having experienced severe trauma need some kind of a release for the stress, or it will turn into anger and rage.

- Don't feel guilty with yourself if you can't talk about the war with your warrior spouse.

- A good relationship will last this period of adjustment. Be honest with your feelings and with each other.

- Do not be concerned it your warrior needs to talk to other Veterans and they happen to be of the opposite sex. He or she just needs to find someone with common experiences.

- Live with HONOR. No one is to blame. War does this to everyone.

2-4 The Pain Inside

- You've got a problem. Face it, and deal with it. Start talking about it with others who have had the same experiences.

- If you start the healing process now, it won't destroy your whole life.

- Start hooking up with the Veteran's Outreach Centers in your area.

- "DO NOT WORRY" about being ashamed or embarrassed to walk into a Veteran's Center for the first time, WE ALL FELT THAT WAY. You don't have to like it, you just have to do it. So do it!

- You are not helpless, and it is not hopeless. Surrender is not in our creed!

- Deal with the issues now, and it won't take you so long to figure out "where" you are going and "how" your life will be in the future.

- If you think you are a danger to your team members, then consider leaving the team. Your life and theirs is far more important than pride or ego. There's no shame in being a human being that has reach the limit.

- You "**WILL**" make it through all the shit. You have the strength of a Warrior to win this battle.

Section Three: Which Way Back to Base Camp?

1. On Patrol at the Mall: Snipers on the Roof!

2. Lock and Load, We're Takin' the Kids for a Ride.

3. Flashbacks: Smells, Sounds and Places

4. Adrenaline Junky

5. Why Scare the Civvies?

6. Who's the Enemy Now?

7. Section Summary

3-1 On Patrol at the Mall: Snipers on the Roof!

On any given weekend, shopping malls are filled with scurrying, wide-eyed people, maxing out their credit cards, and bolting down a barf-in-the-bag hot dog, as they frantically race to the next 10% off sale. And on these crowded days, what you won't find at the malls are many, if any, Combat Warriors.

Why not? You ask. Real simple. We don't like crowds. Even though these are target rich environments, it's nearly impossible to keep track of everything going on around you every minute you're there. To a Warrior, it's a life and death matter to be "Aware of your surroundings at all times!"

I'll explain why your just-returned-home-from-war spouse or partner is nervous as hell going to the mall with you, when he or she is supposed to be "Enjoying your company" and relaxing in the middle of a division of shopping Nazis.

First of all, to this day, I don't like going to malls, or any other place where there are too many people. How many? Well, anything over about 10 to 15 is max. You'll notice how your Warrior's head starts turning a lot more and nervousness increases as the number of people increases. I guarantee that it is not the same when they're back with their units, regardless of the number of Warriors. That's because someone is "watching your back" at all times. The enemy's not gonna sneak up on you and ruin your meal at the chow hall.

When walking up to a mall structure, I always check the roof tops for cameras, unusual objects and snipers. Actually, the procedure is the same for any structure. When walking in the bush (country), the ridge line is of greatest concern.

As I enter the mall, and staying to the middle of the covered walkway (don't know what it's called; don't want to) I make it a point to look back so that I can orientate myself. This is to remember where I entered (what it looks like) in the event I need to leave in a hurry. I also check for barriers (they offer protection under fire) and alternate exit routes. Corners are dark places where an enemy may be hiding. I check every one before walking past.

If my objective for visiting a place like that is to buy something I can't possibly find anywhere else, I purchase what I went in for, and get out as quickly as time permits. Going to a movie is a rare thing. But if I do, it's gonna be the first, mid-day showing since it's less crowded, and the seats against the back wall always seem to feel the safest. That is, unless I go with a "friend." That gives us two pairs of eyes, and the survival rate increases.

Open mall restaurants are usually out, unless I can locate a position with a 360 degree view: a good field of fire. Standard Denny's type restaurants are OK, if while sitting at a counter seat you're facing a mirror to check your 6 o'clock; corner booths are acceptable.

Sounds a little paranoid? No shit! But a person gets use to just about anything over time. And now, as old as I am, this seems like the normal and safe attitude for me. Hell, it's worked!

"You couldn't or wouldn't live like that!" you say. Oh yes you could and would, if you lived in a country where people do snipe at you from roof tops, do rush you with a bomb strapped to their chest, and do attack you from dark corners, while you're trying to grab a little chow. The only difference is, it doesn't happen much in the States just yet. Maybe it never will, but why take the chance?

So you spouses, cut your heroes some "slack", and you Vets, cut yourself a lot of slack. It makes perfect sense to keep doing things that keep you safe. And every time you make it home from the mall, you've made it back from a patrol, alive and in one piece. Seems reasonable to keep up the same tactics, doesn't it? Besides, it keeps you "frosty" (alert).

"Expect the Unexpected!" is an attitude that can bring good things and not such good things across your trail. Depends on the way you're thinkin' about your life. That means, how open you are to change, how grateful and accepting you are of positive events, or how fearful and paranoid you might be. For this Old Knuckle Dragger, it's worked out real well, to be able to smell the flowers and welcome pleasant times, yet keep a round chambered for a snake on the path. Most of 'em had two legs.

But I didn't always feel so good about life. And for a

good many years, I did in fact expect a snake under every bush. Reminds me of a time back in the late 70's. My attitude then, was to carry an olive-drab umbrella wherever I went. Seemed like the Great Bird of "Wake-up-calls," had a real likin' for yours truly. Every time I thought it was safe to come out of the bunker, that sucker had me zeroed-in. Hell, the only way I could have made it easier for him would have been to paint a white X on my head.

You do not have to go through that! But in case you're a bit snake-shy, or afraid to look up, you might just "think," about what you're thinkin'. It does make a difference.

Well anyway, there I was, in the late 70's, in beautiful Boulder, Colorado, tagging along like a stray dog with my first wife. It was decided that our next stop should be one of the best known health food stores in this quiet little college town. Of course, I was well concealed as usual. No long-haired, shit-throwin' enemy of the time was gonna get this Jar Head in his cross-hairs. I blended right in, with my short trimmed beard, sun glasses, hat, military field jacket, jeans and jungle boots. Yep! They couldn't pick my ass out of a line up in the Psycho-Ward.

Boulder was a quaint little town in those days, and after a nice stroll along the main drag, and a slight tug on the leash, we came to our destination. It was about what I expected, a freak show from Barnum and Bailey's Circus. Checking the roof line, and the guitar playing peace-lovers sitting in front of the store, I walked up, stepped over a body, and entered the land of fruits and nuts.

My orders were to locate a kind of horse-feed-type cereal that tasted like dirt with raisins in it. Think it was called granola. Anyway, while sorting through the feed bins and looking at the "Save the Whales" and "Save a Tree" posters (guess saving Tibet wasn't in style yet), I noticed the usual "He's gotta' be a pig" glares from the local "Bong" Club.

Had my under-cover disguise failed? Nah, couldn't of.

Still feeling secure, that my true identity hadn't been discovered, I was also feeling frustrated by not being able to complete my assignment. Then I thought, "maybe the clerk could help, if he wasn't stoned?" but there was no clerk in sight. There was however, a small round bell on the counter, so I walked up, tapped a couple of times, and waited.

There were a couple of small tables in front of the large glass window next to the door, so while I was waiting, it was somewhat entertaining to watch the acid freaks picking tofu burger-crumbs out of their beards and rolling dessert in Zig Zag papers.

Finally, the clerk walked up behind the counter, and while smiling behind a display of Dr. Bronners "All-in-One" Soap, asked if he could help me. He seemed pleasant enough, and not a very large man, but oddly familiar. After discovering that the breakfast feed was over by the squirrel food (trail mix?), and walking back to pay the bill, it dawned on me just why this clerk might be so familiar. After paying the bill, my curiosity got the best of me. I always needed to know my enemy, to be aware of my surroundings, but could this possibly be happening in Boulder, Colorado?

His accent sounded too close for comfort, so I asked him if he'd ever been to Vietnam. "I was born there," he replied, as a little surge of adrenaline cranked into my veins. Then he asked, "Were you ever in my country?" "Yes," I said, "I was touring with the Marine Corps near Chu Lai." Nodding his head slightly, he replied, "Oh yes! I know that area very well." Then he looked right into my eyes and said, "I also was touring Chu Lai, but with the N.V.A." (North Vietnamese Army)

For a moment, time stopped, as we just stared into each other's soul. Yes, we were both Warriors, and yes, a short time ago, we were enemies. Feeling completely off guard, and confused, I said the only thing that I was feeling at the time, "I'm glad the war is over, and we both made it out alive."

A faint smile formed at the corners of his mouth. Then with a sigh, he held his hand out to me. I also reached out, and in that moment of peace, two Warriors shook hands. Not only had we stood on common ground in war, we also stood on common ground in the knowing of the consequences that war brings to every Warrior. Without a word being spoken, we completely understood each other.

We both nodded as a sign of respect to each other. And

as I turned and left the store, I remember thinking, how this man was once my enemy, but in fact, he was a Fellow Warrior, and that "I respect him far more than these hippie trash that are supposed to be Americans". I never went back to Boulder, Colorado again. One traumatic experience like this in my life was enough.

So what's the point of all this, you ask? The point of all this, my Younglings, is that it's perfectly alright to stay alert at all times, to expect the unexpected at all times. And even then, you may be surprised at the bends in the trail. And if you Warriors catch any flack about acting a little different, just remember that **You are different**. Also remember the "I don't give a shit" philosophy.

Besides, would you really want to be like everyone else again? Next time you're in a super market buying chow and checking for points of escape and evasion (exits) look around at the people in line with you. Sometimes it still shocks the hell out of me.

As I'm checking everyone out for possible weapons, general posture, and attitude, I'm amazed by the number of dull expressions, lack of awareness of their surroundings, and the way they slowly push their carts up to the check-out. A dumb-ass sloth could move faster in putting its groceries on the little black moving belt! Damn! Talk about the living dead! Somebody please pull the pin, or at least crank off a few rounds!

And you think you've got it bad? I tell you my fellow Warriors, I'd rather walk around a little shy of a six-pack any day, with all of my "Challenges" (yuppie, shrinker term) than fall in step with the lemmings (small rat-like creatures).

There is nothing wrong with being aware of your surroundings at all times, and prepared for the battle that may never come. Hell, who else is gonna do it? Besides, unless you're low-crawlin' down the middle of the mall, no one's gonna notice anyway. It'll just be your twisted little secret. So "Why Not?" These are all good and useful Warrior Skills. Don't be ashamed of them, and pretend you don't have'em. Oh, and in case I didn't mention it, they will always be a part of the **New You**.

So improvise, overcome, and adapt. You'll be happier.

Let's move out again! We've got some business with the Little People up ahead.

All you need to do on this next mission, is "observe" and be honest.

3-2 Lock and Load; We're Taken the Kids for a Ride

One fine spring morning, your wife and kids decide they'd like to go for a ride with Daddy. They haven't seen Daddy in a long time. Daddy was far, far away, killing people and blowing shit up in the desert. Daddy was at something big people call a war.

Even though you're very busy sitting in your favorite easy-chair, staring at a blank TV screen, wondering why you can't even muster the motivation to get up and take a piss, you agree to the last thing in the world you'd ever choose to do at that moment.

Since you're still sitting around in your skivvies (underwear), because when you woke up, you could barely get out of bed, you now decide to get your ass up and finally get dressed. Walking over the closet, you select a nice, cool, short-sleeved plaid shirt. Then, after slipping on your camo trousers and combat boots, you reach into your duffle bag, grab your K-Bar, a couple of mags of ammo, and sling your M-16 rifle over your shoulder.

You're finally ready to "move out," and while muttering "Oh shit!" you turn toward the door only to find that the whole time you've had an audience. Much to your surprise, your wife looks totally pissed off. You can tell because she's biting her upper lip. Then one of your kids, looking up at Mommy with a confused and pleading expression says, "Mommy! Mommy, what's wrong with Daddy?"

Then Mommy looks down and says, "It's alright, sweetheart, Daddy's just having 'another' bad day". As Mommy looks at you, there's no doubt that any second a white phosphorous spotter round will hit your exact position, to be followed by a napalm air strike.

You're a bit slow on the draw, but finally realize you're in deep shit. And after getting dressed for the second time you carefully place your rifle and mags back in the closet. Giving your weapon a gentle stroke on the barrel and explaining how you'll be right back, you check to see if you're alone. With no one in sight, you cleverly slip your K-Bar in the small of your back, and quickly hide it with the bright colored parka that Mommy bought as a welcome home gift. No one could possibly expect you to go out unarmed!

As the happy family pulls out of the driveway, and heads for the beach, Mommy doesn't talk to Daddy, in fact no one talks to Daddy for the rest of the trip. The kids just keep staring at you like as if Daddy just put five rounds in Big Bird.

This is not a made up story, and this kind of repeated scenario destroys both families and Warriors alike. The fact is, that Mommy still loves Daddy. It's just that she's got the kids and her own life to think about, and Daddy's not thinking at all.

Let's look at what's really going on in this situation. But before we do, both wives and Warriors need to face one real ugly fact. If the wife can't stand it, the relationship is over. If the Veteran won't admit there's a problem and start to work on resolving it, the relationship is over. Either way, "The Kids Suffer." All that kids know is that Daddy went away for a long time. But before he did go away, he loved Mommy and loved them. In their minds, Daddy just has a cold or the flu, and will be OK real soon.

If any of you came from a broken home, like I did, you remember how the fights between your parents caused you such tremendous pain. And as is usually the case, the kids take on the full responsibility of the break up. If you are not "Honest" in explaining what's happening, and "Honorable" in the way you're doing it, then the kids are gonna feel like most, if not all, of what's happening is their fault.

All I'm saying here is, if you can't resolve your differences peacefully, don't dump it on the kids. If you don't know how to explain the weirdness going on, then get some professional help that does. And if you both need some separate space for a while (or for good), make sure the kids understand. Kids don't read your minds, they read your actions. I don't like the word hate, but I do in fact hate to see children suffer when they're caught between two adults who should be acting like adults.

And you Warriors get one thing real straight, and I mean "Listen UP!" There is no option on this one. If you have any of the symptoms of traumatic stress, you have a "Problem." And you can only stick your head in the sand for so long, before it bites you right on the ass. Face it now, and no shit, it still hurts. But it's a hell of a lot easier than waiting like I did. This book is to help you identify your problems, see your options, and ask the right questions. Then if you work at it, make something of your life. And your family is part of that life.

Now, let's get back to our story. First we'll take a look at what's really happening while Daddy is spaced out in his Lazy Boy, then we'll consider what Mommy's thinking about all this. By the way, this is based on many conversations over the years, with many Combat Veterans, and many of their wives.

Plain and simple, the Veteran is in shock. **His or her system is absolutely overloaded.** Think about it. One single traumatic, life and death experience can possibly screw up your life, maybe change your personality, and/or the way you look at most things from that point on.

Some of these Warriors returning stateside have been in combat many times, been on numerous patrols, and have seen heart-wrenching events for an entire year! Some have even gone back for a second (and now third) tour. Can you imagine being in 50 near-fatal car accidents in a year? How about every time you went to the airport, for some reason, you were bumped off your flight, and each time the plane you were scheduled for, crashes and everyone on it was killed? How about you have a family get-together, and when you get back from a quick trip to the store, every single one of the people you loved is dead? Are you getting the picture yet?

The point here is that many of our Veterans now returning home, have been through **multiple** traumatic events; any one of which, without treatment, could be enough to fry their brains for a life time. Hell, I'd still be flunking underwater basket weaving at the "lobotomy club" if it weren't for the counselors at the VA.

Why do you think the shrinkers call these effects, "Traumatic Stress"? The word "trauma" means "an emotional wound or shock, that creates substantial, long lasting damage, often leading to neurosis." (Looked that up for you, no wonder they get the big bucks?) And people wonder why most of us aren't center of bubble?

91

If Americans now, choose to ignore the "Truth", deny the reality that our young warriors are emotionally wounded, and take no responsibility for the wars in Afghanistan and Iraq, they are no better now than back in the days of Vietnam. That would truly be a disgrace for this Nation, and dishonor to Her Children.

But I would like to think that this country has come a ways in forty years. That being the case, it still takes a bit of "intestinal fortitude" (guts) to admit that **right at this moment, our men and women "are" being brutally killed, wounded, maimed and psychologically damaged for the rest of their lives.** By the way, any idea who's gonna pay for all the treatment these Veterans will need? Billions a year, just for the PTSD (Combat Stress) alone.

I'm not here to preach the "whys" of war, I'm here to tell you about the "effects" of war. But every citizen in this country better realize one major fact, and I mean "deal with it right now!"

The Damage is ALREADY DONE! Our Young Veterans are already traumatized for the rest of their lives. And here's a "scary" thought for you. That means, that there are thousands and thousands of well trained Warriors, "Just like ME", walking around with people "Just like YOU!" and you can't tell us apart from the "normal" ones. That should get you up off your ass and streaking to the medicine cabinet for a Prozac.

Here's another grim truth. Once the troops finally do get back, the already crowded Veteran's Outreach Clinics will be overrun. In case you'd like to find out more about this, just talk to any of the administrators at the Veteran's Administration. Talk about needing some meds, these guys are fully panicked over the troop return, whenever that happens.

So now that we know a little more about why Daddy is fried, let's talk about Mommy. This comes from the "heart to heart" talks with not only my ex-wives, but from many of the wives of other Combat Veterans as well.

I use to think, "Man, I wish things were different," and "Why can't I be like everyone else?" Like my Old Sarge use to say, "quit your bitchin', shit-for-brains. You can wish in one hand, and shit in the other, then see which one gets filled up first."

Ah, these true and wise words, spoken to guide his children. Guess I should have listened better to Old Sarge, because wishin' didn't help any of my relationships. I certainly found out which hand got filled up first.

Now, for the ease of writing (hard task for Marines) I'm gonna stick to the man and wife examples. That's the KISS theory. You know, Keep It Simple Stupid.

So what's the wife thinking, you ask? Well, first and foremost, if there are kids involved, you can bet your ass she's tryin' to figure out if a .38, a 9mm, or a .45 caliber pistol is her best option. It isn't often that any "good" mom will voluntarily place her children in harm's way. If the Veteran becomes a risk to the children, you can bet he's history, and so is the relationship.

That means ,Warriors, if you scare your wife with all your stories and crazy actions, or look a little too glazed over for comfort, you'll be packin' your duffle bag and headin' for the street or over to your buddy's base camp. Been there, done that. So you see why I've said, find another "Combat Vet" or a person with similar experiences. You may need to talk over why you screwed the pooch with someone who understands.

The more you try to explain how "normal" you are to your wife, the more you tell her about the war and all of your experiences, trying to convince her that you're really a "good guy," the more desperate and wack-o you sound, and the more disturbed you look in her eyes. With every new story, and every crazy action, you are giving her another **real good** reason to give up on the relationship.

The women I've talked with never stopped loving their husbands, and never doubted that their husbands loved them. They just began not to like that new person any more, or got burned out on the repetition.

Why, you ask? It's because they saw this new person in their life, not trying to get a handle on his problems. To the wives this meant no happiness in the kid's future, and no happiness in their future. That meant no future at all. Living on their own, as a single Mom, no matter how difficult, seemed a hell of a lot better than living with a psycho who loved them.

93

Not a pretty picture is it? Then again, I'm not trying to make you feel warm and tingly inside when you need to look at some real bitter realities. Think about it, and decide what you'll do with the knowledge. Thing about knowing something: once you do, you can **never** not know it again.

Well, after that topic, the next one is gonna seem like a walk to the chow hall.

But stay "frosty," you never know what might bite you in the ass on the way!

3-3 Flashbacks: Smells, Sounds and Places

A short time after being married (to my first wife), my in-laws decided to drop in on the happy family and spend a few days. That was OK, because I had plenty of money for beer at the time. We had just moved to Ocean Beach, San Diego, and lived in a tiny, two bedroom duplex, about a thousand feet from the water. If I remember right, it was only about $300 a month, and even though it was a little run down, it was still about the nicest place I ever lived.

There was nothin' better to me than getting up before sunrise, throwin' on my sweats (and jungle boots), then going for a good run along the beach, before goin' to work. I still don't know if the in-laws were coming to see "us," or just wanted to spend a couple days in paradise. At night, you could hear the waves, and besides reminding me of guard duty at China Beach, it was a great way to fall asleep.

They didn't know me very well, and knew next to nothing about my rifleman's experiences in Vietnam. They had never brought up the subject, and I sure as hell didn't want to talk about it.

One morning, after they arrived, I had the kitchen duty, and was fixing breakfast. Our little kitchen faced the street, so we heard most of the traffic goin' by. This particular morning, my wife and her mom were sitting at our little table, enjoying a pleasant cup of coffee. Their position offered them a clear view of yours truly, working away at not breaking the eggs while burning the toast.

Without warning, a car back-fired right in front of me! **"Incoming!"** I thought, as I hit the deck!

Not thinking anything of the street noise, my mother-in law turned her head, looked into the kitchen, dropped her spoon into her coffee, and without taking her eyes off of me, asked her daughter, "UH, Honey, why is Andy laying on the floor and not moving?"

And no shit, there I was. Pressed to the kitchen floor, like a crab in the surf-zone, waiting for the next sniper round, and wondering "Where the hell is my weapon?"

Having already explained far too much to my wife about the "war" experiences, she calmly turned to her mother and said, "Oh, it's OK mom, he's just having a flashback."

95

"There is no way I can slither out of this one," I thought, and "no one is gonna believe I just dropped down for a quick 25 before the eggs were done," then finally, "Nope! My ass is in the sling for sure." So feeling embarrassed and like something the neighbor's dog just left on our sidewalk (you know, nice and fresh), I got up, went back to burning breakfast, and tried to fit in with the "normies."

In case you're not familiar with the term "Flashback," I'll explain just what that means to me, as well as other Vets. It is also important to realize that flashbacks happen to everyone, all the time. If you hear a song that played when you were a kid, your brain may "flash back" to that time and recall some particular experience that was either pleasant or unpleasant. When you revisit a place after a long time, you remember (flash back) to how it was when you first visited there, and either good or not so good memories pop into your head, and so on.

For someone who has had traumatic experiences, the same thing happens. A near fatal collision at an intersection causes you to flash back every time you pass through it again. Seeing old pictures of the Twin Towers brings you crashing into memories of that tragic event, and floods you with your own personal psychological repercussions (big shrinker words).

The same thing happens with Veterans, only in some cases, the degree of intensity is strong enough to "hold" you in the memory for a considerable length of time. You actually believe that you are back in the jungle (in the desert?) dodging bullets, and hunting for the enemy. There were times in my early years of dealing with this stress that I would stay in a flashback for almost an hour. In my twisted brain, it was like a closed-loop movie, rolling the same scenes, over and over again.

If you don't get this "reaction" under control, it is possible to actually "stay" in the flashback for a considerable length of time, maybe for good. It all depends on each person's willingness to accept "where they now are." I'll explain that a bit.

If you are completely overwhelmed, stressed out, pissed off, depressed, confused, and frustrated with where you are in the present, in order to "survive," you welcome something from the past. Even if the past was painful, your brain picks out a time when you didn't have to deal with so many emotions all at once. It's a sneaky little sucker; it brings you back to a point just below the pain threshold of the present moment, just enough to make it seem a little better. Then maybe, like it did to me, the brain throws in a good memory or two. Kind of like a carrot in front of the donkey.

It is very difficult to describe the actual feeling during a flashback, but I'll give it a shot. Most people have heard of, or have actually experienced what is known as a "panic attack." That's a nice way of saying, that one or a series of events, has just turned to shit, it keeps getting worse, and you are at your maximum limit of control (Prozac time?).

In the Marine Corps, when conditions reach this point, in our limited vocabulary (and favorite words), we simply say that a series of events going bad is, or is becoming, a "Cluster Fuck," or to describe the situation in its conclusion, a FUBAR "Fucked Up Beyond All Reason." Do you see how Marines have mastered a few simple words to describe so many wonderful events?

A flashback creates a very unsettling feeling in your head. First of all, your blood pressure feels like it's off the charts, your heart is pounding so hard, you're sure it's gonna give out at any second. And depending on the kind of experience you are "reliving," the adrenaline is also kickin' in a bit. Maybe the adrenaline is doing the whole thing, hell, I'm no doctor, all I know is how the damn thing feels.

Now, this is the scary part. You are looking out through your eyes. You have to in order to move through the landscape, avoiding trees, holes, and small creatures. So a portion of your senses "is" in the present moment. But, the expectation of the past, "coming into" the present is so great, it's like living "in" two separate events at the same time. That is, in the same exact moment.

For example, on one occasion, when I was caught between two worlds for a period, I was walking through the woods with my M-14 "unlocked" and loaded, thinking "engage and destroy." I knew that I was in the woods, near my home, in the outback of Ohio, and yet I expected the Viet Cong to be walking down the trail at any moment. It was so real that I felt like I was actually back in the war.

The next scary thing is that I also felt that at any moment I was actually going to lose my mind completely, lose control, and "not get out" of the nightmare. That was usually the critical breaking point for me, and what pulled my head back into the "real" point in time, that place in the present moment. Other Vets have had the same experiences, and the main factor in maintaining a small measure of sanity (or insanity), is our strong commitment "Not to Lose Control." We know what we're capable of, and do not want to unleash that on innocent people.

In extreme cases, when a Veteran does cross the line into the past, and stays there, he knows he may be walking in the woods, or down a trail, but that's where reality stops. He believes he's seeing bamboo trees or palm trees, and the trail is barbered by rice paddies. Now-a-days, it might be an oasis in the desert.

When I was an honored guest at the VA Hospital, Psycho Ward, I talked to other Warriors who were disturbing, even for me. These guys were so far gone, and they "jumped" back and forth so much between the painful present and the Flashback Loop, that they really weren't sure what was real and just a bullshit memory. Not a good place to be.

In all truthfulness, in the story of when that car backfired (and that situation happened a lot), I was actually more comfortable flashing back to my old unit, my true friends, and the life I understood, than being a confused, dumb ass on the kitchen floor.

To me, combat with friends was a hell of a lot better than where I was. Sure we were pissed off and frustrated there too, but at least we could go out and burn something down, blow shit up, or shoot at somebody. We had a way to "release" (Shrinkers call it venting) our anxiety, our emotions. We also had other Warriors next to us that shared the same feelings, and over a good drunk we could talk about it. Even if all that "venting" wasn't carried out in the most productive way, it still made us feel better.

"So what do I do?" you ask, and "How long will it take to handle these flashbacks?" The answer to the first question ain't rocket science. What "you do" is, you accept the **fact** that there just might be a problem in your dip-shit brain that's causing you to have flashbacks in the first place. And damn it! It's not your fault that you do! Remember, you are a feeling human being. You weren't designed to experience what you did, and not be affected by it. So cut yourself some slack, there's nothing wrong with the way you're reacting.

Now here's the good news. The more you talk about your flashback feelings with other warriors who have had similar traumatic experiences, and the more you participate in professional counseling at the VA, either one-on-one or in a group, the milder and milder the flashbacks become.

Why you ask? It's because, just like riding the emotional surfboard when you're dealing with loss, you have to learn to "turtle" under the wave that each flashback dumps on you. Same-e-Same. The more you **accept your present life**, the less your brain can trick you with flashbacks from the past. The more you deal with your traumatic problems, while learning to improvise, overcome and adapt to your new life, the more "you like" the present, and don't need to go back in time. With good professional help, it won't take you as long as it did for me, to get the flashbacks in a very manageable place in your brain-housing-group.

OK, the answer to the second question might sting a bit. But I wouldn't really call it real bad news. It's sort of like going out to take a ride, and while you're making a flight check on your car, discover a flat tire. You know the "Oh shit" comment.

Fact is, after more than 35 years, I still stop and track a Hewie (old type helicopter), remembering sitting in the door and flying over rice paddies. The smell of burning grass still reminds me of torching villages with my friends, and taking fire from the "little" snipers. **It never really goes away, because I don't want it to.** What! Man, this Jar Head really is whacked! you say. Well, maybe so, but just hear me out, before you stick your head up your ass.

The reason I "choose" not to forget all the bad stuff, is because it's mixed up with the good stuff. When you accept who you are and what you've become, and that you actually "did" a **Damn Fine Job** at being a Warrior, it's like turning down the volume on a radio. I've learned that you Youngins now call radios, IPods. I call'em I-puds (ask a marine on that one). Well anyway, as you turn the volume down lower and lower, it becomes more like background music. It's not so loud that it prevents you from thinking of something else. Just like going into a nice restaurant and having dinner and a cool one. You hardly know the music is playing. And after a time, you can barely hear it anymore, because after a time, you're feeling better about yourself, and the life you're living through in the present moment.

You now have a future, and you've learned to live with the past. Enough said.

OK, let's get on down this next trail. Watch that ridge line for enemy movement, and stay frosty!

This one may cause a bit of concern.

Being fed up with my dip-shit friends, and a family in denial, like I mentioned, I returned back to base before my 30 days of leave was up. I had my fill of civilian life in about a week.

Walking into the Headquarters' office at Camp Pendleton, California, and handing my orders to the clerk, I noticed a few Marines standing off to one side. One of them, a sergeant said, "Hey Marine! You got the balls to try out for Force Recon?" I looked over and asked, "What do I have to do?" He replied, "Just don't quit!"

My thoughts were very clear on this new opportunity, and my small green brain started to tingle with the thoughts of a chance for some excitement. Less than a month ago, I was hunting Charlie, and callin' in artillery strikes, and now in almost no time at all, I was already bored shitless with Stateside duty. "So why not?" I thought.

Having the illusion I was in good shape, we began running up a hill, and then down the same hill, repeating this clever tactic until in fact, several Marines did drop out pukin'. They always wanted a few drop-outs in the first hour or two. And over the course of this continuing "test" of our moral fiber (which seemed never ending), and my initiation into the 5th Force Reconnaissance Company, I became "hooked" on the possibilities of the training ahead.

Today, the new "buzz" words are Spec. Ops. This means Special Operations. And by the way, where do you think all those writers in Tinsel Town (Holy-woody) get all the catchy little phrases to throw into their fantasy action movies? Yep! It's from all the Old Knuckle Draggers and their Young Pups, that's who. You know, the military.

What Spec. Ops. means is that warriors go through and continue with training in a wide range of schools. Everything from languages, to jumping out of airplanes, repelling from helicopters, rock climbing, scuba diving and learning about the newest weapons and explosives on the list. Very exciting topics for someone looking for a good adrenaline rush, and I was "their man" in line for the needle.

"So what's the point of all this?" you say. The point is, that in a little over a year, I went through 52 weeks of schools and training, and "not one" of them ever came close to the adrenaline rush of combat. Scuba diving, jumping out of airplanes and helicopters, having submarines sink under you, rock climbing, and blowing shit up, just didn't do it.

"And the point still is?" What I'm saying here, is that adrenaline is as addictive as any drug, and you don't get it with a needle. You get it from being **scared**. The super "hit," comes from being in a life and death situation, and living. It's just that simple.

The more you think you might die, the more adrenaline pumps into your body. And for a short while, you feel stronger, faster and more alert each time it does. Ever wonder why people like the roller coaster, the "fairies" wheel, or the twirl and puke rides at the amusement park? Same-e-Same. The only difference is that you're pretty much assured you're gonna make it off the ride alive and in one piece.

The "Bottom Line" is **Fear Equals Adrenaline**. The more danger, the closer to death, the bigger the rush. Some people like horror movies to get a tiny adrenaline hit from being a bit frightened, a few Vets like combat movies to reconnect to the rush of battle. It's all the same, just varying degrees of intensity.

So now you're asking, "What's wrong with skydiving, scuba diving, rock climbing, or bungee cord jumping?" Well, there's nothing wrong with any "controlled" sport that has a degree of safety built into it for the doers and/or the looky-loos. You wouldn't normally go skydiving without a safety shoot, scuba diving without a back up or buddy, or bungee jumping without a rubber-band strapped to your ass, would you?

When the need for adrenaline does become a problem is when you're driving 90+ MPH in heavy traffic, hunting "hunters" during their week to play Rambo, and putting unsuspecting citizens in danger just to get your fix. Been there, done that, and I regret to say, a lot more times than I care to talk about.

Like any addiction, adrenaline causes you to do things that you would normally not consider. It is a way of escaping and makes you feel more alive at the same time. However, the problems that develop for Veterans (or anyone) in these times of searching for a way to distance themselves from trauma-caused pain, is that you're dealing with more than one source of stress at the same time. And since I've lived through it, I'll explain this problem as I see it.

Let's suppose that in fact you're rollin' down the freeway on your motorcycle, clocking along at 90 mph, weaving in and out of traffic. You decide that by knocking on the driver's side window of a sporty little car, you'll surely impress the fine looking girl behind the wheel. But when this beautiful young lady shows how much she admires your bald head and combat boots by flipping you off, and yelling obscenities, you decide to go even faster, and be even more reckless. "That wasn't so bad," you think. You still have your bike and five bucks for a few burritos at Taco Bell, but you **were** rejected. Even that's not so bad. But the real problem is, that's not all you're dealing with in that moment.

What's happening here (and guess who was on the bike?) is that by riding the motorcycle recklessly to get a little rush of adrenalin, innocent people are being put in harm's way. On top of that, the rejection lowered the level of self-esteem even more, and added to the already high levels of stress to the Veteran.

You'll have to remember that Combat Warriors just returning from war are often "overwhelmed" by emotions they don't know how to handle. There is most likely guilt, the anguish of remorse, the pain of loss, survivor guilt, etc. Basically you're brain-fried, like if someone just clamped a microwave dish to your skull.

This is where it gets a little tricky for the Warrior, and a little dangerous for those caught in the blast radius. If your focus for the moment is getting a real good rush of adrenalin, and you know that the closer you get to death, the greater the rush, then you're pushing the envelope to get all you can. Trouble is, while you're doing 95+ in traffic, getting your hit, the other traumatic waves of emotions may decide to surface at the same time, and kick you right between the legs. If that happens, as it did to me, that telephone pole, concrete barrier, or oncoming semi-truck gets more and more tempting as a way to end the pain.

My choice always seemed to be to live, but on one

occasion,, I guess the Archangel Gabriel was riding on the back of my bike, because I "just" missed a car that didn't see me coming so fast. And there "just" happened to be an off-ramp, as I almost dropped the bike, but was able to gun it upright, pull off and into a nice green park that "just" happened to be there, before I shit my shorts. I've never believed in coincidence, and this finally drove the point home.

I got off the bike, and while shaking like I'd been in a freezer for an hour, sat on the grass, and wondered how I could have possibly made it through all that uninjured. I sure as hell got my rush of adrenalin, but I almost caused a major accident as well as killing myself in the process. That last incident proved even too much for my slow-on-the-draw thinkin' to ignore. I never did that again. And I hope you'll learn from this example of what NOT to do.

By now, you're probably wondering, "So what's the solution?" And once again we ain't launchin' the Space Shuttle here. When you finally begin to **like** yourself for being a decent human being, who only acted like a Warrior is supposed to act, and you start to gain some **self-worth** (you know, self-esteem), you no longer need the "fix" of adrenalin. That's because the other traumatic problems are also becoming less of an issue. It's like an onion. The more layers you peel off, the smaller the whole onion gets, and the less gas it makes when you fire it down.

As you peel off each layer of traumatic stress, everything gets easier to deal with; you've lightened the load in your back pack. And if you haven't gotten the picture yet, most of your improvement is going to happen as you improve how you look at "you"! Now remember, I'm not a bull-shitter. It's gonna take some work, but like I keep sayin', you are not alone, and you sure as hell can make the grade.

Rest assured Warriors, if you read this book, and you're honest with yourself, and you still screw the pooch, it's your choice. You can do like I did in the past, and feel sorry for yourself for years, until your disability becomes your identity. Or you can do like I finally did, and take a chance on "sticking your head up under fire", then get on with your life. You decide if your tomorrow will be exciting and filled with promise, or the same dark nightmare you've been living in until now.

Surrender is not in our Creed! Improvise, Overcome and Adapt! Gut it out, until the new you, creates a new life, and just the way you want it!

Now, let's break camp, and move out to the next topic.

We're among friendlies on this patrol, so be at ease. (But I've still got your 6 O'clock.

3-5 Why Scare the Civvies?

Recently divorced from my second wife (in Ohio) but still on good terms, she invited me to a pre-Hallow-wiener party, in October. It was actually a monthly get-together where all the gals that cooked would select a certain country, then make dishes from that region. You know, like Chinese food for China, and Italian food for Italy. Well, on this particular occasion, the ladies had selected Vietnam! And my ex said "It's a come-in-costume event, be creative."

Oh boy! My somewhat out of balance brain-housing-group went into double time. Then she said "We'll be featuring Vietnamese food." Ooh Rah! Even better yet. I told her I'd have to pass on the dog burgers, but I 'd be sure to be there.

Since at the time, I was making military spec. Ghillie suits (bushy-burlap sniper suits) for the Spec. Ops Community, I decided to go as a sniper. What could be better in my green mind? I thought, than a Marine sniper at a Vietnamese party.

The fact is, I'd had a lot of time in the bush with snipers in concealment tactics, and was an instructor in escape and evasion, so I felt right at home in my Ghillie suit. I'd spent many hours sitting motionless among the ants and other delightful creatures, watching unsuspecting folks ditty-bop by.

Just as a point of interest, I've made hundreds of Ghillie suits for Warriors all over the world. But back in the days of Vietnam, when I took out sniper teams, we did the old break-off-vegetation routine.

In the late 90's I was asked to develop a lightweight, military spec. off-the-shelf suit for select operators in the community, which I did. Working closely with the Alphabet Agencies, my wife and I were the only ones (as far as I know) allowed by the State Department to send Ghillie suits "out" of this country.

"Wife?" That's right, my third wife! I always got a kick out of the fact, that this wonderful little "Peace Maker" made the best Ghillie suits in the world, for the fiercest Warriors in the world. She made hundreds, and everyone was perfect.

So what's the point you ask? The point is (to add to your concerns), a trained Spec. Ops. Sniper, with a Ghillie suit, is about the worst nightmare you could ever imagine. If he went psycho, that is. And you just guess how many there are right now in these two wars. Well anyway, back to scaring civvies.

I arrived at the party early, low crawled up to the front steps, and laid in position as the guests arrived. One by one, they strolled by and into the house, completely unaware that a somewhat disturbed Marine was watching every move they made. After a time, I was actually able to slowly roll over, and sit up against the stairs. They still didn't see me!

About the time I was reasonably certain that most of the guests had arrived, I heard someone ask my ex, "Where's Andy?" And that was just what my small green brain was waiting for. Standing up and walking to one side of the door (out of sight), I knocked loudly. The hostess came to the door, and I moved into position, standing dead center in the doorway. Holy shit! What an entrance!

Everyone in the room went dead silent. All eyes fixed on the new arrival. And at that moment, all you could hear were assholes snapping shut, as fear streaked through the air like a tracer round. I felt very good about the whole thing.

They were finally able to take a breath as I pulled back the hood to reveal my grease-stick-painted face. "God, I'm glad that's you," was one comment. And "you scared the shit out of me," was the common response from the others.

So why scare the civvies? Real simple, once again. By scaring civilians, it was my way of forcing them to acknowledge the "fact" that I was truly a Warrior. It made them face the "reality" that war creates people like me, who "used to be" just like them.

If I hadn't been the local and friendly Marine in the neighborhood, but in fact was a demented, stuck-in-a-flashback, psycho who just happened to walk in on a Vietnamese party, with a loaded weapon . . . well, you fill in the rest. I can say for sure that it wouldn't have been much of a stretch of the "twin-realities" in a flashback, with people dressed in black pajamas and pointed hats.

Truthfully, it also made me feel "good" for the short time I was laying in the bush, watching all these unsuspecting people. I felt like I was back in the jungle, which was more like home than anywhere I'd been Stateside. It also felt good at the time, because I thought a little harmless pay back was in order for the way some Americans treated us Warriors.

It is also important to note, that as a Warrior, it was (and is today) very critical to establish some kind of identity, some degree of self-worth as quickly as possible, in order to think you fit in "somewhere." I was desperate to feel like I was part of the society that I went to war to protect, and that there was some valuable reason that could possibly justify the sacrifices I'd made.

I had changed, my life had changed, and I needed to believe that it was all for a good reason, that there was some degree of purpose to give me the strength to live through each painful day.

The same is absolutely true of our Young Veterans today. And wait until you hear their stories when they get back from war. As long as no one gets jailed or wasted, it will be very interesting indeed.

On a lighter note, sometimes Vets just like to scare people a little to get them out of their face, maybe establish a little distance. For example, I was at a gathering once, and somehow, a young woman got wind that I was a Marine. Must have been the Harper Valley gossip club, don't really know. Don't really care.

Anyway, she was with her beautiful little daughter. And they both had on the usual hippie dresses, with matching peace signs dangling from their necks. Must have been the family thing to do in those days. You know, those who protest together, stay together?

I was definitely "aware of my surroundings at all times," and remembered my little run in with the "Peace Loving Goddess of Hate and Rage" in California. So I carefully followed her movements as she walked straight for me.

She seemed a little hostile, and I thought, "Oh shit, here we go again." But this time, I didn't want her getting too close. Quickly turning my head, I gave her a serious look.

Guess she had "some" common sense, because she

stopped about four feet away. Then, in this self-righteous, arrogant tone, she blares out for everyone to hear, "I believe in World Peace!" Without a second's hesitation, I replied, "I KILL for it."

I could see her pupils dilate as she took a step back, her body tensing with fear. I'm guessing from her expression, she was thinking "don't piss off the baby-killer Marine." Maybe she was trying to impress the other assholes in the room, but she didn't impress me, as I watched the "Footprint of the American Chicken" quivering around her scrawny little neck.

I was not in the best of moods anyway, and it was fairly obvious that in no way did I want to listen to her ignorant bullshit. Yep! That was the end of "that" wonderful get-together for me. So as usual, I headed for the door, keeping an eye on all of her quivering little crusader friends, and headed for the closest drink I could find.

People didn't really consider how us Warriors felt in those times. They only wanted to cleanse their souls at the cost of ours. And our returning "Young Veterans" do not need to listen to anything close to that crap when they get home! Every single American needs to be proud of these heroes. They have been fighting and dying for their principles and convictions in a war they didn't start, and a war they are not responsible for. If you want to get pissed off at someone, then take it out on those two-faced cake-eating politicians in the Capital Mole Hill, NOT our troops.

There isn't much risk in picking up a sign and walking around with 10,000 protesters. It's a different matter all together to pick up a rifle and die for what you believe in. So if any of you Youngins take any flack when you get Stateside, you just remember one thing: this Old Marine is proud of you, and so is every other Combat Vet I know. We've got your 6 O'clock!

Besides, opinions are like assholes, everybody's got one. Just consider the source, and say, **"I don't give a shit,"** and **"you'll feel better, when they're not around."**

Because that way, you'll feel better about "you," and that's the only damn thing you need to feel at all.

You might want to chamber a round for this next Section.

109

Safeties off, "Spread Out!" and watch that tree line. We're entering enemy territory

3-6 Who's the Enemy Now?

After being "in-country" (Nam) for a time, it became easy to figure out who the enemy was. Anyone who had a pointed hat, slanted eyes and ate rice was Charlie (Viet Cong). By the time you filled your first body bag with the leftover pieces of your Brothers, or saw the heads of your interpreters stuck on poles for your viewing pleasure, you quickly hardened to the fact that "Everyone is the Enemy." That is, if you wanted to stay "frosty" and make it home yourself.

The Geneva Convention was a joke. It was a set of rules for war that only we had to follow. So when we had to chase the enemy across the border of a neighboring country, we'd send in the Korean Marines (ROK's, Republic of Korea). They did a wonderful job and didn't give a shit about rules. I've never had much use for the United Nations anyway, but it would have been nice to have a few "Blue Hats" around when you needed them. At least the Australians showed up for the party. Never met an Aussie I didn't like.

You can't trust anyone in war, except your fellow warriors. Hell, even our barber was a Viet Cong, and got a personalized lesson in skydiving without a parachute. That was our way of interrogating prisoners. Terrible you say? No, that's just the way war is. There are no rules, and there sure aren't any referees or goody-two-shoes calling "foul" or "unfair."

So what's the point, you ask? Don't worry, I'm gettin to it. Just need a little time to warm up a bit.

By the time you arrive Stateside, you pretty much distrust everyone who looks even close to the enemy you were just fighting, and that's perfectly understandable from a Warrior's point of view. The cute little kids you're sharing your meal with are found laying dead in a night ambush, caught trying to smuggle in explosives to blow the shit out of you and your brother's the next morning. How could anyone expect our Vets to feel any other way but untrusting?

What you don't expect, however, is for the round-eyes at home to turn out to be like the enemy you left in war. Maybe you can see how it wasn't (or isn't) much of a stretch for a Combat Vet to take a rifle up on a building and start killing anyone in range.

In this situation, the Veteran felt like his war hadn't ended, and there were no "friendlies." With the right amount of traumatic stress, the right conditions to prove that, in fact, he had been betrayed, he felt that "suicide by combat" was his chopper out. And if he had to go, he'd take as many of the enemy as he could with him. This did happen.

So here's my point. These were tragic events that we as Americans, **do not** want to see happen again. And if we're not real careful, it's very likely they will.

To you Warriors from the Afghanistan and Iraq wars that are reading this book, I want you to understand a few things very clearly. There **ARE** friendlies now. There **IS** help for you now. Your true support base is your fellow warriors, and the old knuckle dragger like me. I'll be damned if you're gonna' go through what we did, with or without the support of the American public.

And I hope like hell that the American people of this great nation make some amends for their disgraceful actions to our Veterans from Vietnam, by treating our new young Warriors with the dignity and honor they deserve.

And now to you Warriors, I ask this:

"Who is the Enemy now?"

The answer to this, my Brothers and Sisters, is that if you are now among people that love you, and you're in a country that honors you, then that only leaves one enemy left. That enemy is **you**.

This is a tough hill to climb my friends, I've been there. And it means that you'll really need to look deep inside if you're gonna' find any answers that fit. No two humans are exactly the same. You will all feel different degrees of pain and have different limits for dealing with it.

There are many common experiences in war, but when it comes to dealing with those experiences, it's up to each of you to choose your own path to your own future.

You **can** do it! You **can** make it! And you **will** have help! You'll just need to **ask** for it.

Enough said on this subject. Now! You'll need full

body armor for the next section. Remember my Younglings, "You don't have to like it, you just have to do it!"

Let's lock-and-load. We're movin' out!

Section Three Summary

3-1 On Patrol at the Mall; Snipers on the Roof!

- Being aware of your surroundings, at all times, is good!

- If your tactics for survival worked in war, they'll work in peace.

- It is normal for you to be vigilant.

- You act different because you are different.

- Remember the "I don't give a shit" philosophy.

- It's better to be Brain Fried, than Brain Dead.

3-2 Lock and Load, We're Takin' the Kids for a Ride.

- You can't hide from yourself. Deal with it, you've got a problem.

- Your family is more important than your ego, or your bullshit macho attitude.

- Communicate with your kids! If you can't or don't know how, then find some professional help that does, and do it quickly.

- Traumatic events have traumatic effects on you. It's "normal", and it's OK to feel what you do.

- There are hundreds of thousands of you right now in the PTSD Boat. Don't let it sink!

- This country needs to face the consequences of the wars in Afghanistan and Iraq right now! Not repeat the apathy and denial of Vietnam.

- Children come "First" in the family. They are just small adults. They understand your "actions", not necessarily what you say. So don't act like an asshole.

- Moms will protect their kids first. Show your ass and you'll be out on the street.

- If you don't get professional help, the relationship is history. It may already be too late.

3-3 Flashbacks: Smells, Sounds and Places

- Flashbacks are normal, just don't stay there.

- It's OK to want a comfortable place to go.

- "Accepting" that there is a problem helps. Doing something about it, helps more.

- Time and professional help will lessen the intensity of flashbacks.

- Flashbacks never go away completely, you just get better at dealing with them.

- When you have a future, you'll learn to live with the past.

3-4 Adrenaline Junky There is no rush like combat, so deal with it.

- Fear produces Adrenalin.

- Looking for an adrenalin fix, can be dangerous to you and to innocent people.

- You are probably already overwhelmed by high stress. Stop for a minute and "think" about what you are just about to do. It may save your life.

- Stay on guard, because suicide can be very easy in times like these.

- When you feel good about yourself, you won't have to push yourself to the brink of Death.

- You "will" be able to discuss this adrenalin problem when you get some help.

- You are not alone. You have back-up. The old Vets are covering your 6 O'clock!

3-5 Why Scare the Civvies?

- Accept yourself as a warrior, you don't need anyone else to do that for you.

- No one will understand the reality of war, unless they've been there.

- Self worth comes from Self-Respect. So respect yourself for being a Warrior.

- What you've done, will certainly scare people. Be sure you want them to know that part of you.

- You fought for your beliefs and convictions. Bare your pain in silence to those who "will not" understand. Speak only among Warrior "friends", of the things that only Warriors can know.

- Don't hate those who do not understand. Just feel better when they're not around.

3-6 Who's the Enemy Now?

- Its normal for you with your experiences to distrust. Trust must be earned.

- There are friendlies here. You just have to know where to look.

- You are your own worst enemy.

- The choice is up to you and you alone. You have the strength to make it to a better life ahead.

Section Four: Can Anyone Hear the Pain?

4-1 Psychiatrists: Full of Help, or Full of Shit

Many a combat Veteran has sat in the padded-leatherhead- shrinker's chair, recounting the nightmares that haunted their every waking moment. I was no different. But on my one and only visit to Dr. Bafoon's office, I just couldn't get past watching him casually jot down a few notes, as I poured my guts on the floor, and sat there screaming inside.

I wondered if this idiot had misplaced his padded helmet, and actually heard anything I had to say. All the little nods, the "Uh Huhs," and the "How do you feel about that?" were really starting to piss me off. For a few minutes, the thoughts of my own problems shifted to thoughts of aggression toward the good doctor. I thought "this jerk-off is a waste of air, and if I'm gonna' start flushing the toilet of humanity here in the States, this puke-for-brains is my first tug on the handle."

Quickly realizing that, in fact, I had come to Dr. Do "Little" for help, and not to body bag his sorry ass, at about the next "How do you feel?" I'd had enough, and replied "Look Doc! How the fuck do you think I feel?"

"Oh! No need to act out anger here," he said, while tensing up and sliding his chair around behind his fancy large desk, and I'm sure also noting "passive aggressive," or just plain aggressive on his brain-pad.

Taking a controlled breath, as I was "slipping the safety off and pressing the trigger" in my own mind, my final comment was " OK Doc, let me put it to you this way. Did you ever kill your neighbors kids? Then, blow away your neighbor's cute-little, fluffy-white dog? Then burn down their house for the hell of it?"

"Oh my God NO!" was his reply. "Then we're done here," I said, "Because you don't know squat shit about **How I feel!**". As I got up and left the quivering little puke, I was thinking, "if I took a good shit on his shiny, organized desk, I wonder how he'd 'feel' about that?"

It didn't take long for even my deep-fried brain to figure out that I was getting more help from a good bottle of wine than from idiots who hadn't shared the same Warrior experiences. My friend was right, I truly did need help. But I had no clue where to find it, until an unknown thought swirled in my green mind.

So on one especially disgusted day, I asked the Commander and Chief! I said, "God Sir! Is there anyone who knows jack-shit about what I'm goin' through?"

And when you ask, you receive! My friend called, and had seen something about a Veteran's Outreach program on the TV. "Thank YOU, God Sir!" This was the answer to my prayer in hell.

Now I was able to talk to someone who "walked the walk," and didn't have to look up PTSD in his Thomas Guide for Wackos. And as I began to attend the sessions, I could see that it truly was an uphill climb all the way, but there was finally daylight peaking through the end of the rifle barrel.

It was in fact, very amazing (Marines are amazed easily) when I found out that there were many Warriors just like me. These Veterans had infiltrated into every walk of life. And unknown to the civilian population, these Warriors were trying to fit in, yet all of them were walking time bombs. There were police officers, firefighters, cooks, corporate executives, bikers, and just plain crazies like me. It was like walking into a secret society where everyone had two identities (Marines: not two sets of teeth), and it made me feel part of a Brotherhood.

During that period, except for medical personnel, most of the veterans were men, caught between self-destruction and a world they no longer understood. I knew I was in deep shit, but this Center was my life boat, and finally, somebody was throwing over a line to pull me out. Little did I know, however, that when I began to work with the Veteran psychologists, they would eventually save my life.

Having read this book so far, if you fit any of the symptoms, it might be real smart to visit your local Outreach Center, and have a chat with the Counselor. There is no shame in having a traumatic stress disorder. Remember, it's the natural reaction to traumatic events.

If you're single, you may have a little time (not much). If you're married or sharing your life with a partner, **do not hesitate.** If you're married and have kids, **do it yesterday!**

It doesn't hurt to walk in and say, "Gee-wiz, since I got

back from war, I'm having nightmares, cold sweats, depression, panic attacks, fits of rage, remorse, flashbacks and thoughts of suicide," and, "do you think there's something wrong Doc?"

No shit Sherlock! Another no-brainer! And look, it doesn't mean you're off to the Leper Colony. Your conversations are private, and no one is gonna' know you're meeting with Mrs. Thumb and her four daughters three times a day.

My fellow Warriors, no one is gonna' feel your pain, except someone who's been through what you have. And YES, I do feel your pain. I do understand what is burning you out. And there **is a road to recovery**.

Now once again, I'm not gonna' bullshit you. It's **not** easy, it's gonna' take time, and you are going to need to work damn hard at it. There are going to be nightmares for a time, flashbacks for a time, and all the other little piles of shit in your head that need flushing.

You can either start right now, to work on a new life, or you can do the dumb-ass thing I did, and feel sorry for yourself, deny your feelings for years, and wait until the trauma of your experiences kills you, innocent people, or someone you love. The choice is yours.

But your Old Sarge is tellin' you right up front, "You're not alone on this one", and if you're not afraid of a little forced march with a heavy back pack, and full combat gear, then "Get your ass up, and move it out down the trail!"

Hold onto those weapons for a bit, cause I'm gonna show you a path you **don't** wanta' walk down.

Let's head over to the next topic.

4-2 I'll Just Kill Everyone Who Pisses Me Off

Living on a mountain top in the outback of Ohio was good for me (I thought), but sure wasn't hunky-dory for my neighbors. Being Mennonites and pacifists, they looked at me like something that had just crawled up out of the Valley of Death to test their faith. Don't get me wrong, they were nice enough folks, and were constantly "praying for me" as they would say, but treated me like the lost soul on the block. At that time in my life, guess they may have had a point.

Recently divorced from my second wife, I'd built a nice little house on **My** mountain, complete with a flag pole. And looking up at Old Glory and the Marine Corps flag, as I returned from work each day, reminded me of "Marlboro Country" back in the Nam.

Once every couple of months, on a weekend, and much to my neighbor's delight, I would have a "shoot." That is, I would gather all the crazies I knew (like attracts like) who would all bring beer, food, and lots of ammo, then we'd shoot the shit out of targets all afternoon. What were the targets, you ask? Well, that was the real fun part, and since I was sort of in charge of creativity, I always tried to make things interesting.

Besides the usual human-size silhouettes, I'd go to the surplus store, buy some BDUs (combat clothing) stuff them with bundles of newspaper, then stuff a ski-mask for the head, and spray a nice big red star on their chest. You see, we were getting ready for terrorists and didn't even know it.

After we'd blown the mannequin all to hell, and my honored guests would stagger home, I'd go hang the dummy in a tree, on a rope, by its neck, next to the No Trespassing signs. This was for the viewing pleasure of the hunters that conducted their sweeps near my little command post in the forest. Interesting thing was, as the population of dummies increased on my fence line, the trespassing decreased as well. Imagine that! "A little twisted, but not so bad," you say?

All this seemed fine with me at the time, and besides I could have always used a few more prayers headin' my way.

But the dummies on the fence line weren't really the problem for the trespassers, it was the Dummy that lived on the mountain with the flag pole. And for the first two hunting seasons, there were "almost" a few more enemy bodies hangin' around the camp site.

When I was shooting the mannequin (Marines: not a man that can), I was shooting the enemy all over again. And when the unsuspecting want-a-be mercenaries showed up, they actually became "live targets." That's right! The first couple of hunting seasons were not a pleasant experience for anyone within range.

When the hunters began shooting at the deer that I had befriended over the past year, I began to shoot at the hunters. Not to kill them, since I "did" realize there weren't any pointed hats on their heads, I just intended to scare the shit out of them, which I surely did. Besides, it didn't seen quite fair. They were all dressed up in their "bright orange" hunter's fashions, and I was in a Ghillie suit. Not much thrill in that, not much of an adrenaline hit either.

Something that easy would have been like side-swipin' bicyclists goin' up a hill. You know, the shit-for-brains, arrogant assholes, in their shinny bright leotards with the padded retard helmets, that think they own the road?

Well anyway, the point I'm tryin' to make here, is that besides a few hunters that had their assholes snapped shut as a .308 round cracked just over their heads, many more of them were **"in my cross hairs."** And that's not something hangin' out of your nose. It's the two black, vertical and horizontal lines in a rifle scope.

I truly can't remember the number of times I was lying in my Ghillie suit, with normal everyday people in my sights, a live round in the chamber, the safety off and slight pressure on the trigger. I wanted to pull that trigger so bad, and if they had given me any excuse whatsoever, I'd have killed every one of them.

Are you a little confused yet? That's understandable. So allow me to shoot up a flare, and shed a little light on the subject. And you young Warriors listen up! I'm already seeing killings on the evening news. And you civilians listen up as well. It's starting already!

Last night, it was reported that a combat warrior from the "new" wars, ambushed two unsuspecting Police Officers. During the firefight, the Marine advanced under fire, and

123

needlessly killed both of these fine men. The news-cast went on to explain that the Marine was part of a gang prior to entering the Corps, but that makes little or "NO" difference whatsoever. That explanation was just a desperate attempt to explain away this senseless killing. The concern and fear of both the reporting officer and the news-casters was obvious. And they should be concerned and afraid. Why the hell do you think I'm writing this book?

Now, let's get back to the point of this spooky topic. If I was going to therapy, getting a grip on survivor guilt, loss, rejection, etc., and discovering the new me, why the hell was I ready to shoot innocent people? Well, since I'm baring my soul, and my most twisted thoughts in this work, at the cost of possibly losing the few associations I may have developed, and so that you young Warriors don't duplicate the Old Sarge, I'll tell you.

After this, some of you might say, "We need a website for all Combat Vets! We need to know where they live!"

Funny thing is, not being real hi-tech, I'm sort of an M-14 , K-bar kinda person. So when I first heard the term website, I thought it was where those nasty little black bugs lived. You know, the ones that have silk twine comin' out of their ass.

But those of you with great concern about the "Warriors Among You" may rest assured, because the Department of Defense knows where most of us live. Or at least they're suppose to.

When people have asked me one of the usual "stupid" questions, like "Why do you have a 100% rating for PTSD?" I usually say, "it's not because I've killed so many people, it's because I want to **continue** killing people". Almost every time this has happened, I could see their pupils contract to pinholes, their respiration increase, and a definite shift in their body language. They were afraid to be near the Warrior, when the Warrior told them what he was really thinking.

What they actually wanted was a nice rational sugar-coated answer to talk about at the breakfast club. I've used this tactic many times, to get rid of people that bore the hell out of me, and it works. Trouble is, it's true.

In combat, in a firefight, in a kill or be killed situation, when you do kill an enemy (fellow Warrior) there's a definite sense of satisfaction. It feels real good to know "that one isn't gonna' crawl up on your position ever again." For a seasoned warrior, in a justified killing, you don't feel guilty, in fact you feel relieved. It's like, "One down for good, next batter up, and pass more ammo!"

I've had many good friends in law enforcement who know exactly what I'm talking about, because "we've" talked about it. Maybe they say what has to be said to internal affairs, because their careers were on the line, and maybe their necks on the chopping block. But they know the feeling of a "Good Shoot.". They just can't admit it to everyone. And these guys are heroes, every day! When some puke-breath, shit-eatin-meth-head just offed a kid for a fix, and turns his weapon at you with a glazed-over, insane look in his eye. Damn! I couldn't pull the trigger fast enough! This person was truly a waste of oxygen, and definitely qualified for extinction.

Those of you who are of a less timid nature, may say, "So what's the problem?"

Well, once again, it's a little more of a problem than meets the eye.

Since returning to this country in the 60's and going through the rejection, denial, criticism and anger pointed in my direction, I felt then, and feel exactly the same today, that if I've killed people I respected (Viet Cong), how much easier would it be to kill people I don't respect, and even hate? The answer is real simple: "Real easy".

Once again, the people of this country better wake up and fast! Write your cake-eating congressperson or senator, and support your Veterans coming home by asking for money for the Veterans Administration. The trend right now seems to be to cut funding. And if you civilians haven't figured it out yet, we are all gonna' have a "REAL BIG PROBLEM" real fast if we don't get these young Warriors some help right now.

There are at least 250,000 troops (maybe double that number) that feel the same emotions that I've been describing in this book. That means without professional help, there could be that number of skilled Combat Warriors, walking around with you, waiting for the right situation to explode. The Veteran's Administration recently estimated that it will cost Billions of dollars just to deal with the troops now diagnosed with PTSD (Combat Stress) from these two wars. I can think of a number of solutions to this money problem, but you probably wouldn't like any of them, and that's not the reason for this book.

Now, let's return to the "So what's the problem?" remark.

Let's just suppose you're a young Warrior, having just returned from your second, third or fourth combat tour in Iraq, honorably discharged and out of work. You're lying comfortably in your Ghillie suit, holding a beautiful Model 700 sniper rifle, and have the target in your cross-hairs.

You have no prospects for a job, and don't have the desire to find one anyway. Your wife divorced you, the kids think you're crazy, your head's pounding from the pressure of survivor guilt, and you're half drunk.

At that moment, you sure as hell don't respect anyone, much less yourself, and your chest feels like it's in a vice. And as the trauma of the war floods your brain, you decide that today is the day you end it all.

You make a final windage adjustment, exhale, hold, and slowly squeeze the trigger. Seconds later, an innocent victim lays dead on the pavement. The SWAT team is on the way, and by the time it's over, more people are zipped into body bags.

This is not a made-up story. I only moved it into the present day, and our present problem. We do not want this kind of tragic outcome for our young Veterans.

So let's sum this up a bit. It is more than likely that our newly returning Warriors who have just been killing in war, may want to continue with the killing. It could be for the adrenalin rush, payback, anger, being caught in flashbacks, or any combination of emotions we've been talking about.

Now, they may think they don't want to kill children, and the innocent, but only the "deserving", justified targets. And by justified I mean, putting themselves in situations that gives them any real good excuse to kill for a marginally justified reason. I went out of my way with a loaded weapon on the front seat of my truck, hoping to find some excuse to kill someone "deserving".

If Veterans, caught in these kind of blinding emotional

waves, don't get help right away, the post traumatic pressures may build up until they literally explode. In that moment, depending on each individual, they may not be able to distinguish between the innocent and justified targets. Everyone becomes the enemy, and all hell breaks loose. I hope you Young Veterans are snappin' in on this. I'm pullin' out all the skeletons just for you, and you sure won't see this shit in a training film.

If more and more situations come up like that Marine killing policemen last night, it's only gonna feed public fear. And we saw what that did 40 years ago. We DO NOT want that happening again. It just isn't worth it for you, or for this country.

"OK Sarge, so what do I do about this desire to kill?" you ask.

Well my young friends, that is simple to say, and hard to do. I've been there, done that. So I'm just gonna' tell you how it worked for me. And my address still isn't: Sgt. Brandi, C/O the Wack-o Ward, Fed. Penitentiary. So I guess I'm doin' something right?

And here it is. You get to the point where you believe **YOU and your life is worth more than the scum-sucking-night- crawlers you'd like to waste**. Just that simple. The longer you stay in **one place**, the more you get to know your neighbors, the more responsibility you have (like responsibility for animals), the less likely you're gonna throw all that away to satisfy the urge to kill again.

Now I'm **not** gonna bullshit you. The desire to kill surfaces in any life and death situation, and every time you get really pissed off at someone.

But you can't just kill everyone who pisses you off!

I also think about my Brothers who died saving my life, and how I would certainly let them down if I threw my life away in one single act of violence. You see, you just have to find something that brings you back to the present moment, something that grounds you in your new life.

If you don't feel much self-esteem yet, and can afford

it, maybe saving some little dog at the animal shelter will make you feel better. I've got two of 'em. And these little **friends** will definitely teach you the "real meaning" of unconditional love and acceptance.

Fact is, I take care of 21 farm animals, plus my two dogs and one very old cat. Ya see, I've "upped" the stakes a bit. And these animals have kept me from killing more than one asshole over the years. I'm only telling you this, because for some Vets like myself, people just weren't enough to stabilize the desire to lose it all. People can take care of themselves. Animals need our help.

The word animal, means "Living Soul." And these guys have saved mine. The animals in my life are like being with beautiful innocent children that depend on me every day. They give out far more love than I could ever return. So keep that in mind if you've had a hard time with relationships like I have. You can still have a great life, and simply pick the times you want to be around people. We've got enough to deal with, no need to complicate things.

Now let's get on to the next topic. You'd better still keep that body armor on for this one. But don't sweat it, after what you've already been through, you can handle it.

4-3 Suicide and Homicide, or Honor and Love

Heading back to base camp on a typical monsoon day, we followed a bend in the trail. Just as the rain let up a bit, we could make out the sandbag bunkers with Old Glory hangin' on a pole just guiding us home. We had been in the "bush," on patrols and a search and destroy operation for over 30 days. We were filthy, exhausted, pissed off, and looking forward to our first hot meal since before we left on our public relations tour among the happy little people in our sector. They always enjoyed seeing us, knowing that we had come to burn their village to the ground and shoot all the family members we could find. And besides, it was Christmas, and they certainly couldn't be left off of Santa's gift list.

Passing the check point, we walked up to what was left of the chow hall after a mortar attack, fixed our bayonets, stuck our rifles in the ground (upside down) , grabbed a couple of ammo cans and sat down. Ah, it was good to be home.

Murphy was smiling on us this day (so far) because the weather had cleared long enough for the choppers to bring in ammo and that hot meal we were hoping for. To this day, I remember that wonderful smell of hot turkey and dressing, and there was even something that looked like a biscuit!

We filled up our mess gear (sorta metal plates) with a great meal, and walked back to our festive picnic area, ankle deep in mud. And just as we sat down, it began to rain, monsoon style. For anyone not familiar with tropical monsoons, it's a down-pour so hard that you can barely see any distance at all, and it splashes mud a good ways from the ground back up into the air, especially if you're "on" the ground.

Well anyway, there we were, watching our only hot meal in 30+ days washing off our plates while we tried to fire down a piece of wet turkey and what was left of a soggy, biscuit- type substance. That is, before it all turned to brown slime.

As one after another of us lost the race, and began throwing our mess gear down in the mud, one Marine looks over, and while trying to light a cigarette under his poncho, says "Merry Fuckin' Christmas." As we replied in typical Marine Corps fashion with "Fuck you, I got your Christmas hangin', " and "Here, Merry this, asshole," our wise and "all knowing" sergeant, listening to his children, Speaks! He said, " Listen up you shit birds! As bad as you nose-blowers think this is, it ain't no big thing. Deal with it!" And "All you swingin' dicks are going to heaven, cause you spent your time in hell. And I'll be there to kick your asses if you fuck up along the way."

We all smiled and humbly bowed our heads in gratitude, while the last of our meals washed down the hill. Our "Father Sergeant" taught his pups never to quit, no matter how bad it seems. He let us bitch and blow shit up to release some of our anger, but never, ever quit!

Our Father Sarge did go to heaven on our next operation, so I know he's standing there with spit-shined boots, ready to stick one in my ass if I don't stay locked and loaded on the trail ahead. In the Corps we say, Semper Fi. It means "Always Faithful". "To what?" you ask.

We are always faithful to Code, Corps, God and Country. That is, the rifleman's Code of Honor, the Marine Corps Family, to God, and to the Principles set down by our great Nation. In that order. And country "does not" mean, cake-eating-limp-dick politicians.

Now, applying the wisdom of my Old Father Sarge, one thing is very clear. Suicide is a chicken-shit quitters' way out, and homicide (murder) is breaking the Code of Honor. Doesn't matter how the goody-two-shoes shrinkers put it, it's just that simple to me. Black and White, no Gray.

You know what I mean by gray? You don't? Well, here it is. Gray is indecision! Looked it up, it means not knowing what the fuck to do next, sort of like a fly. "A fly?" you ask. Yep! Just like a shit eatin' fly. Here, I'll give you an example.

Let's say you're a fly, and were just at the Brown Diner, you know, finishing up a good meal compliments of Buffy next door, and you decide to buzz over to the table and piss off some people. Ah, but slumped in his chair, sits a fully alert Marine, firing down brain-grenades (beers) but well trained in the killing of all manner of life.

You smugly land. And instantly, two large gnarly

hands come at you from both directions! Your small, shit-filled brain is confused. "Do I go forward? Do I go backward?" Splat! Your ass is history! The Marine takes a confident swig, and returns to his busy 1000 yard stare. So make a decision, Black or White!

Now, on a more serious note, "What is Suicide?" It's usually a good idea to know the meanings of the words you use. So, in the "Book of Big Words", it says that Suicide comes from some foreign language. Sui means "of oneself", and cide means "to kill". Well, that's OK, but I like this old Marine's definition better. Sui means "Sewer", and Cide means "To one side", as in a turd, slipping to one side of the toilet. Somehow, puttin' it that way makes more sense to me.

When you kill yourself, you're only going one place. That's down the shit tube. Your life is over, and you've just dropped your back-pack. The forced march is over, and you've just quit! And the way I look at it, someone that can't hack it and quits, lacks intestinal fortitude, "Guts". Look, I truly understand the desire to kill yourself. Been there many times. I could say that I didn't want my ass kicked in heaven by Father Sarge and a size 13 boot in my ass, but I've sorta had my ass kicked before and got over it.

"What stopped me?" you ask. It was the fact that I'm not a quitter, and live by the Code of Honor. So what does honor mean? It simply means "Respect". **You must respect (honor) yourself first!** You must respect the ones who love and respect you. You must also, respect your right to live a good and productive life. A life that brings some joy into your tomorrows and the tomorrows of others. **If you're a Warrior, your friends did not save your ass so you could blow it away! So Honor (respect) That!**

And my friends, you cannot just **think** yourself into respect for yourself, you must **Feel** it and believe that its true. " But how do I start to respect myself?" you ask. Well, that one is easy to say, and very hard for some to do. Hopefully you're better at it than I was. And I'll explain some of that for you.

I had to go back in my life and pull out one experience at a time, one quality that I respected at a time. You might consider doing what I did, and actually sit down with some paper and a pen, then make a list. This isn't easy either, because it also drags up all the shit in your life that you don't respect.

But don't be discouraged if 50 things come up you don't like. Only write the ones down that you do like, the ones that you respect yourself for. Pretty soon, you'll have a list of real good things to make you feel better about "you". And if it helps, put the list on your refrigerator or some place that you can look at it all the time. This will remind you that **You Are** an Honorable person.

It can be anything that makes you feel good about YOU. For example, Being a good Marine or Solder, a good Police Officer, a Nurse, or helping someone in need. Maybe you helped someone get through a bad situation, maybe you demonstrated compassion, took in a stray dog or cat, gave someone a ride to the market, or gave a street person a smile and a couple of bucks.

Everyone has done things that feel good and those things made them feel good about themselves. You just have to remember. Hell, if you can't remember enough good things to put a "Happy Face" on your list, then start a daily record of things you do for the "Greater Good". That is, start from today and move forward, marking down every good thing you do that makes you feel better about you. There's an old saying that "You never lose by giving," and "When you do good things, good things come back to YOU."

Here's one "Real Important" thing to keep in mind. Never **compare** your list of good things to anyone else's list. We are all different. We all have different experiences, abilities, and personalities. We all look at life in our own way, so we are not the same as anyone else in the world. We are only **similar** to others. And my friends, we have all made very good and very bad decisions in our lives. The main thing is, we're still alive to think about it. And as long as you "are" alive, you still have an opportunity to add to the positive side of the list.

We have all "Done the very best we could". So maybe you judge other people, and that's up to you. Just don't judge and condemn your Self. The interesting thing is, if you respect yourself, value yourself, and are finally looking at a really good future, why would you not want to be around to enjoy it? Why would you want to kill yourself, or someone else? No situation is worth that. And besides you'd wreck all the plans you've got for the good life ahead!

In some ways, life kinda' reminds me of a voyage I once took on a troop carrier. Sometimes the ride was smooth as glass, with beautiful seas ahead, and other times, it was rough as hell, and I was hangin' over the side pukin' my guts out. Same-e-Same. The better you feel about yourself and your life, the smoother the ocean stays. That is, most if not all the time. "Why" you ask? It's because the little things don't make big waves anymore, and your traumatic emotions don't have a chance to drag you under.

"So what about the ones that have already committed suicide?" you ask. Well my friends, unfortunately, I have known more Veterans who have killed themselves than I care to think about. And I do understand the feelings of wanting to end the pain at any cost, of not seeing any way out, any relief other than death. Why each of us chooses to live is our own individual choice. In the final roll call, you're gonna' have to be the one to decide if you're still here to answer up "Here Sir!" to your Creator, or if you've decided, with your own "Free Will" to not trust that you had some useful purpose for your life.

I would also like to say to those who have lost loved ones to suicide, that it is not my "intent" to criticize or shame those who have chosen this escape. And keep in mind that death by suicide is **Not the fault of anyone living!** I have seen situations where family, true friends and true loved ones, made no difference in keeping the gun from the Veteran's mouth. There was nothing I could say, or anyone could say, when the "Will to Live" was lost. At that point, they just had all they could stand, and saw no relief in sight, no hope for a better life ahead. But what I'm also saying here is, that with some good professional help, and a lot of strength, **which you have**, killing yourself becomes less of an option. The less pain you feel, the less critical you are of yourself, the more you'll be willing to stick it out a little longer. So why not live until tomorrow to see what happens? And then the next day and the next? You've got nothing to lose, and everything in life to gain.

Eventually, as you gain self-worth (value) and self-esteem (respect), that is, finding the good things in your life that make you feel good about "You", there will be a threshold that only you may choose to step over. It is a junction point in your journey, a place where you decide that rather than choose Suicide and Homicide as a path to your future, you choose to live by Honor, and to Love living life for what it truly is: an opportunity to be grateful and joyful for every moment well lived. And living every moment is something you don't want to miss!

This all make sense to me, my young friends, because "I Am Here" to tell you first hand, that it works! And if this Old Jar Head can do it, then damn it, so can you! That about wraps up the mission for this section.

So let's saddle-up, climb aboard the choppers, and do a little aerial recon. Your tour's about up, and it's time to get back in the "World" , and get on with it.

You know, the **New You**, in the new life.

Section Four Summary: Can Anyone Hear the Pain?

4.1 Psychiatrists; Full of Help, or Full of Shit?

- Find professional help with "like" experiences.

- Stop in at the Veteran's Outreach Center in your area.

- Counselors can save your life, and get you started on your new one.

- There is no shame in having a traumatic stress disorder. It's being human.

- Feeling pain is normal. Deal with it and it will get less intense; ignore it and it will get worse.

4-2 I'll Just Kill Everyone Who Pisses Me Off

- Innocent people are not the enemy. You are your own worst enemy.

- If you put yourself in a dangerous situation, you may just pull the trigger.

- Don't transfer killing in war, to innocent civilians that piss you off. It isn't the same, so don't make it the same.

- There are thousands of Veterans with PTSD. You are not alone, and now there is help.

- Your life is worth more than anyone who you "think" deserves to die.

- Killing is necessary in war. Don't make it murder at home.

- Staying in one place a long time seems to help many Vets. Get to know your neighbors, and if you can't stand being around people, maybe adopt an animal or two.

- Pick the times you want to be around people. Don't get over-loaded with stress by being too sociable if that's not what makes you feel better about you.

4-3 Suicide and Homicide, or Honor and Love

- Suicide is a quitter's way out, and homicide is just plain murder.

- Live by a Code of Honor (respect) for yourself, and for other good people.

- You have a Right to live a good and productive life, and to experience happiness.

- Your "Friends" did not save your ass so you could blow it away.

- Everyone makes good and bad decisions, and everyone does the best they can at the moment.

- Each day of your life is an opportunity. Don't just throw that away. Give it a chance, because with the right attitude, life can be better than you ever dreamed.

Section Five: When the Going Gets Tough the Tough Get Going

5-1 A Tribute to Nurses and Doctors: Heroes All

The temperature was well over 100 degrees and the humidity seemed about the same, as we briefly rested in the shade of the grass hut we hadn't burned down yet. There were a few of us that hung around "Doc" most of the time (if we could) to make sure he stayed as safe as possible. "Doc" was actually a Navy Corpsman, and medically trained to take care of Marines in the field, and in combat (no small matter). In the Army, a person with these same types of skills is called a Medic. You can call him whatever you want, but we called him Doc, and as far as we were concerned, this man could walk on water any time he wanted to. He never did quite get the hang of changing rice paddy water into brewskies, but we forgave him for it.

The "little people" had gathered around us in sufficient numbers to prevent the resupply of food and ammo, so we exercised great caution in selecting targets and ate our c-rations sparingly. Enemy activity had stepped up considerably at that time of the war, so we didn't want to risk the lives of the pilots or their helicopters unless it was absolutely necessary.

It was the third day after our food ran out, that a chopper finally "streaked in" under fire, and dropped some ammo. But no C-rations. The pilot had a really fine pair of brass ones. You know, balls? And we figured he was either single or just got dumped like most of us by that time.

It was easy to tell the difference between married pilots and single pilots when we called in an air strike. The single pilots would come in so low that the front edges of their wings would glow blue. They'd drop their ordinance, hit their after-burners, and blast out of sight, tail-end toward the ground at such an angle it was almost like saying "Kiss my ass!" to Charlie. The married pilots wouldn't come in so low, but they'd still "do the deed" and blast out of sight as well. Couldn't blame'em for wanting to stay alive, or not ending up in the Hanoi Hilton.

Anyway, we were glad to be resupplied with ammunition, and by that point, clearly understood the saying that, "when you're hungry, you'll eat just about anything." Talking about what kind of great chow we were gonna have when we got Stateside really didn't help much, in fact it just made us more hungry. But then it happened!

Out of the tall grass appeared a Duck! Mind you, this wasn't any ordinary duck. This small, pathetic creature looked like it had just been med-evaced in from Bangladesh on a bad day. But it surely didn't matter where it came from to us. And using our superb survival training, we pursued this small winged lizard until it was finally turning on a stick, over a fire. Trouble was, not knowing squat shit about survival, we used a somewhat dried stick for a skewer, which of course burned up quickly and dropped our precious carcass into the coals. It still didn't matter, "cause we were dining in style!"

I don't know if you've ever eaten rattlesnake, but this feathered lizard was about that bony, less tasty, and a whole lot greasier. The point of all this is, as hungry as we were, Doc was given the lion's share of what little there was. We had to force him to take it, but eventually, the smell of bone, gristle and a few burnt feathers got the best of him. He was unquestioned in anything he chose to do, and we couldn't do enough for him. He was "the Man" and our hero.

Of course the duck kicked our asses in the end (literally). We all got worms, and amoebic dysentery (screaming shits). And I'll be damned if a chopper didn't drop us off some food about 6 hours after our gourmet Bar-B-Q!

The man we called Doc was our dearest friend, and our greatest hero. He only carried a .45 caliber pistol and a full pack of medical supplies into the field. This man would stand up in a firefight, without any regard for his own life, and run to help a wounded Marine,. We all knew that if we got hit, Doc was on the way! And when "Doc" moved out, headin' for a Marine, we'd increase our rate of fire, and at times, offer ourselves as a target to insure his safety. Doc was not only our Hero and our friend, he was a man we loved and would die to protect.

Whenever we got back to a real base camp, with real nice (hard back) tents and a chow hall, Doc would always get the first swig of rice wine (or whatever it was?) and the first hit on the Bong. There was always one around, from guys returning from Bangkok, Thailand. And yeah, we smoked weed and hash whenever we could get it, as long as we weren't standing guard or going on patrol.

What do you expect we'd do? After coming in from the battlefield, we sure as hell didn't sit around cross-legged humming with a crystal, or taken a vitamin pill (or valium). You needed to kill a few brain cells after a combat mission, anyway you could. And you'll have to realize, we didn't think we were coming back anyway, so who gave a shit about a healthful diet?

We were told then, and I'd venture to say it's the same now, that in a full blown firefight, a machine gunner's life expectancy was under 10 seconds, a rifleman's wasn't much better. Not good odds for a plane ticket home (in a seat).

Well anyway, after a few fingers of fake whiskey and a few hits on the bong, old Doc would start breaking down a little. This man carried a lot more baggage than we did, and we were about ready for the basket weaving classes in the local psycho ward. Doc felt guilty for every Marine that died in his arms, every single human being he couldn't save.

We tried to comfort our Hero as best we could. We'd say to our friend, "Look Doc, when a man's guts are blown out, or his legs and arms are ripped off, and you can't get in a med-evac, you can't possibly save him with a few field dressings and a little morphine." But nothing we said seemed to make any difference, and he just kept drinking to cut some of the pain.

It usually ended with our beloved friend passing out from exhaustion and booze, with a stream of tears running down his face. We'd roll him into a mosquito net, hoping he'd finally get some rest and maybe for a short time, a little peace. But after the next patrol or a major operation, the whole thing repeated itself once again.

Our Hero, our Friend, our Doc, never made it home. He died on the battlefield, doing what Warriors do, giving up his life for the brothers he loved. He lives in my heart now, and after more than 35 years, I can still see him smiling as he was biting into that scrawny duck leg, laughing about our lousy cooking skills. He made a difference in my life, just like the Nurses, Doctors, Corpsman and Medics are making a difference right now in Afghanistan and Iraq.

I know an Ex-Military Nurse today, a 100% PTSD

Veteran, who still can't get the ghosts out of her head. Hundreds of men died on her watch, and many in her arms. She remembers every one of them, and everyone of them took a slice of her soul as they parted company for the last time. She still lives the nightmare, and is one of the strongest human beings I've ever known.

Day after day, the wounded would roll in, and the body bags would roll out, filled with the ones that couldn't be saved. She felt **all** the desperate emotions of the men she tried to save, and the reality of just how helpless she was to stop their deaths. She then carried her guilt, her loss, and these tragic memories with her when she returned Stateside. And the trauma of that war, of that loss and of that guilt, haunts her to this day.

I see this happening right now to these wonderful men and women overseas and in the medical facilities here. Their only fault is that they Love. They Love Life, and understand how delicate a thing it is, but can't prevent it from slipping away from our beautiful young Warriors.

I cannot tell you in words how much us Old Warriors respect (Honor) you Peace Makers/Medical Warriors for what you are now doing. Not only do we Honor you for "who" you are, we love you for unselfishly sacrificing your lives for the lives of others. That's right, you now offer to all those you care for, the "Ultimate Sacrifice" , and will live with the consequences of your loving actions for the remainder of your days. Doesn't matter what the price is you have pay, you'll do it regardless. It's just the kind of person you are. And each of you will always be our "Doc".

To you my friends, my heroes, I can only say this: **please** do not hesitate to seek out some good professional "like-experience" help, and the sooner the better. I cannot, nor will I pretend, to understand the depth of your loss and guilt. Your job is to save lives. Mine was to take lives. And with the numbers of men and women now returning from field and hospital assignments, either in or related to the wars in Afghanistan and Iraq, I suspect you will find more than enough fellow Veterans to form your own Civilian/Military "Talk-it Out" groups. Only others having experienced exactly what you have, will understand exactly how you feel.

Once again, Thank YOU!

Over the course of about 10 years, when I was making military spec. Ghillie suits, I came into contact with a lot of law enforcement officers on the Special Weapons and Tactics units (SWAT). These brave Warriors are fighting the scum bags of this country, up close and personal, to make it a safer place for all of us. Law enforcement is very much like the military in many ways. That's one reason why so many Vets put on the shield, and go back into the bush, so to speak.

It didn't take long to figure out, even for this Old Marine, that these guys were dealing with some (if not most) of the same issues I had with traumatic stress, and they weren't getting much help in working it out. So what else is new?

Most people can see how being in law enforcement, fire fighting, emergency rescue, and medical services can cause Post Traumatic Stress. No shit, even if someone's brain-housing- group was operating in first gear, they could figure that out. But what about Mr. or Mrs. "Normal?" You know, the ones in the dwindling middle class, climbing up the corporate ladder, take the kids to soccer, "do your home work" kind of folks.

Oh Boy! There are assholes snappin' shut all over the legal drug cartel on this one! Forget peddling hard-on meds to the old folks homes! Let's get our new TV ads goin' on the PTSD freaks!

I can see it now. "Got PTSD?" Take one of our new FDA approved pills! You may experience dizziness, limp dick, heart failure, vomiting, explosive shits, and the hair might fall off your ass, but "man you'll feel great!" You and all your zombie friends can put on your padded helmets and ride from pisser to pisser on your mountain bikes. And by the way, you can guess at what a Marine can come up with for the letters, FDA. Be creative.

"So what about Mr. and Mrs. Normal", you ask? Well let's suppose you're driving along with the kids in your 5-Star, crash proof mini-van on your way to the land of the Golden Crotches. As usual, the kids are fighting over who gets the last gummi-bear, or some other stupid-shit-thing,

143

and the day so far has really pissed you off.

Earlier that morning, half asleep, you opened the front door, only to find your neighbor's dog shitting on the daily news. He was trained "on the paper," so what does he know? But you don't care about his affection training, and just missed him with your shoe! Only trouble is, you didn't miss his thoughtful gift on the newspaper, which ended up dead center on the bottom of your foot! Limping back into the house, you notice a flat tire on the car, while your neighbor is giving little Buffy a doggie treat. Ah, life in sub-burbia.

In your mind, the day has turned into what was sticking to the bottom of your foot, you've had it with the brats in the back, and you're thinkin' about that hidden bottle of Jack Daniels in the closet. The traffic is heavy, but you turn around to yell anyway, not noticing you've just run a red light and the semi that's just about to T-Bone your van!

Everything goes into slow motion. The kids had unfastened their seatbelts during the argument, and the air bags couldn't protect everyone from the impact and multiple rollovers. Somehow you made it out alive, and wake up in the intensive care unit. Afraid to ask, but needing to know, you hear what can't be true. You're the only one alive!

Now, let's look at this tragic event with what we know about traumatic stress disorders. Remember, first of all, you are a human being, and you're suppose to "feel" emotions. And riding in automobiles is not a natural thing, anymore than skydiving or bungee-chord jumping. We've just gottin' used to it, and it beats walking across the country or putzing along on a horse.

I've talked to people who were the only survivors in an accident, and they needed professional help like all the rest of us, and in some ways, maybe more. But the one thing they need to face right away, while the trauma of the experience replays in their head, is the "I'm responsible, it's my fault" feeling.

Sure, in a war you feel guilty too, but Warriors can blame it on the war. Civilians in these kinds of situations often have nothing to blame it on but themselves. And if you are a sole survivor, you're still gonna go through many, if not all, of the same symptoms that a combat veteran does.

Besides the trauma of the actual physical and mental

experience, you're going to feel the "loss" of loved ones. You may feel survivor guilt if everyone else died and you didn't. You may feel the guilt of responsibility and you'll sure as hell have "flashbacks." You will most likely go through cycles (waves) of emotions, such as anger, guilt, depression, blaming everyone, or just yourself.

You will feel pain in your chest, pain in your head, and you may even consider suicide, or start doing things that are reckless, hoping you'll die. You may consider illegal drugs or start drinking alcohol to excess. But one thing is for sure, you've got a problem, and it's a **normal** human reaction that you do. So cut yourself some slack!

There is nothing weird or strange about your reactions, so it's not time to go out and pick out a grave site, or make out a will. And I don't give a damn how young or old you are, if you're alive, then life can certainly be worth living. If you've read the book this far, you can see very clearly that Post Traumatic Stress does not play favorites for the military alone. Any traumatic experience can change your life, and can force you into dealing with emotions you didn't even know you had.

It's like I've been jackin'-my-jaws about with these Young Vets, it's not an easy road for anyone, and it may take a lot of work, but you "can" do it! And if the pain seems too great, and you can't find any way out but suicide, remember what I said in that section. Just wait until tomorrow, just to see what happens. And then tomorrow, just wait until the next day, and live one day at a time. Go at it easy.

You may want to change your whole life, and that's OK. Maybe that's the way you'll find a new start, maybe a little peace, and a way to begin to live again.

Now, let this Old Jar Head give you a new and improved Marine definition of PTSD. You are gonna have to **"Improvise"** to solve new problems in your new life. You're gonna have to **"Overcome"** obstacles that may seem beyond your limits of strength, and you're gonna have to **"Adapt"** new tactics to bring yourself into a positive, creative frame of mind.

To me, PTSD means "**P**sychological **T**raining for **S**elf **D**iscipline!

And remember this. You are ""NOT" the same person

145

you were before the trauma you've experienced, you never will be, so **let the "old you" go bye-bye.** In other words, shit-can it. You can't hang onto it anyway, and it will make you miserable to pretend, so what have you got to lose?

Your traumatic experience will also be with you for the rest of your life. And with a little help and time, it will no longer dominate your every waking moment. Eventually, it will be much easier to deal with. You don't give into it and you don't get rid of it, or forget about it. **You just allow it to be that part of your life that doesn't ruin the rest of your life.** And the rest of your life, can be the "best" of your life. A future that you make just the way you'd like. So "Gut" it out! And "Greet the unseen with a cheer".

You need to **Adapt** the list of PTSD affects to your own life, and get some professional help. Because once you're comfortable with yourself, and "respect" yourself, knowing that you're a damn good human being, and you've done the very best you could, the "Joys of living, will be the life you're living". And no shit, I'm here to tell you it's possible! If I can do it, anybody can.

Alright then, just **"Suck it up"** and let's move out to the next topic.

5-3 Why Do I Have PTSD?

"Stand up, Hook up, Shuffle to the Door, Jump right Out and Count.....Oh shit! My chute's not opening!" is how I felt for years. If your parachute isn't packed properly, and all the little cords get twisted up, and the canopy doesn't open, then you have what used to be called a "Cigarette Roll". That means your ass is headin' for mother earth for the "big kiss," and real quick like.

In this situation, you've got two choices. You can release the main chute while praying that your reserve chute wasn't packed by the same dip-shit, or you can ride it out and do an exceptional "parachute landing fall": that's a five point landing that's suppose to take up the shock of impact. Unfortunately, I saw this happen while I was in jump school at Fort Benning, Georgia. Never heard what happened to that trooper, but he decided to ride it out, all the way to the ground.

So then, over the course of about 8 years, while seeing my ass streaking toward the entrance to the "Happy Hunting Grounds", I needed to find out some of the answers to some of the big questions. And with the point of impact getting closer all the time, I thought I'd give organized religion a shot.

Marines don't half step on anything, and I advanced under fire with a 100% effort to find out what all this book learnin' had to offer. I read everything I could find: the Koran, the Bible (didn't know there were so many different ones), all the Eastern stuff, and anything I could lay my calloused hands on.

Then one day, I read about this warrior type guy named Siddhartha Gautama. Most people know him as The Buddha. And he made a lot of sense. Well actually, he was sorta' like Jesus, in that he never wrote down anything. They had their fire-teams (privates, lance corporals), writing down all the stories of where they went and what they did. By the way, Jesus and Mohammad weren't timid souls either, and sure weren't afraid of goin' on patrols into enemy territory.

All the books seemed to say about the same thing: Know Yourself. Well no shit, I thought, that's what I'd been tryin' to do. They also said that God is always watchin' your

6:00 O'clock. That worked for me, too (learned that in the foxhole). But hell, watchin' Crocodile Dundee when he said something like "Me and God, we be mates" made about as much sense as most of the stuff I read. And through most of it, nobody talked about "dealing" with the shit you've already been through, except Mr. Siddhartha.

The ass-trologers said it was your destiny, and the planets and stars caused all this to happen. Some people talked about Karma and how all that made things happen. But the Buddha reminded me of Old Sarge. He said, "Look you dumb shits, if there's an arrow stickin' in your ass, don't worry about the texture of the wood, or the bright-little-winged- lizard feathers at the end of it. The damn thing is stuck in you, so Deal With It!"

And once again, that small green light glimmered in my cluttered brain. I realized that I sure as hell had a PTSD arrow stuck in me, and I'd better pull out the shaft and deal with healing up as best I could. The point of all this is simple. **If you've got a PTSD arrow stuck in your ass, you'd better learn to deal with it. You may always have a scar, you may always limp a little, or feel the wound on a cold day, but it's "not" gonna ruin your life unless you let it**.

So here we go! "Why do I have a Post Traumatic Stress Disorder?" you ask. Well maybe it was the planets, fate, karma, Murphy, or any other excuse you'd care to make, but the fact is, **You've Got it.** And it's gonna stick with you like a tick on a dog. Like it or not, you are damn well gonna have to deal with it now, or deal with it later. I recommend now.

Alright then, my fine Youngins, let's look at what may have caused a round to jam in your chamber. As you go through the list, see if any of these hit the "bull's eye," and you don't have to say a word to anyone (unless you need to read out loud like Marines). This will be your own little secret for now; you can say "Holy shit!" in silence.

Do any of the following fit you?

1. You have been through a traumatic, "life and death" experience, maybe a lot of them.

2. You may be feeling "No one understands me." That may be true unless you talk to the right people.

3. You are in "pain," mentally, physically, or both, and you don't know why.

4. You are suffering with the emotional waves of "Loss."

5. You are feeling "helpless" in getting a grip on the waves of emotions flooding your thoughts.

6. You may be feeling "survivor guilt," because you are still alive, and your friends are not.

7. You may be feeling "guilt" over the things you've done and don't know who or what to blame.

8. Nothing "seems the same" to you anymore. Everything that was once familiar, comfortable and normal is now different and uncomfortable.

9. Nothing feels important, not family, friends, work, nor your life.

10. You are not sleeping much, and having nightmares when you do.

11. You are having "flashbacks" from your traumatic experiences.

12. You want to return to the war, to your unit and friends and don't really know why.

13. You now have a violent temper. You get pissed off over every little thing, and want to lash out at everyone all the time.

14. You may want to kill everyone who pisses you off. Everyone is an asshole.

15. Your guard is always up, and you can't trust anyone anymore.

16. You can't seem to find any real friends to "trust."

17. You can't relax around people, and can't stand crowds.

18. You can't go into public places and not be on full alert, checking for the enemy.

19. You've turned to drugs and or alcohol to kill the pain in your head and body.

20. You've lost what self-esteem you once had, and don't think you're worth squat shit.

21. You can't make plans for tomorrow because the present is so miserable.

22. No one wants to be around you anymore, not family or friends. You've become angry, hateful, critical, and negative about everyone and everything.

23. You may be thinking of suicide as a way to escape, and have become reckless with your life and the lives of others.

24. You feel like no one gives a shit about you anymore, and don't have a clue why.

25. You find it more comfortable on base than around civilians, or you just want to be alone all the time. The 1000 yard stare has become your pastime activity.

26. And generally, you're up to your neck in shit, and nobody's throwing you a line.

Well, my fine troubled friends, no matter how many of these nasty little items have struck a chord in your brain-housing-group, it's not hopeless, and "I AM" throwin' you a rescue line. So rest assured. And you may still smell like shit for awhile after you get pulled out, but don't sweat it, you'll meet others that smell the same way. Once you shower up, you can rub a little deodorant on your ass, and no one will know the difference.

This is just an Old Marine's way of saying **You Are**

Not Alone. There are ways to get through all this, and **YOU WILL improvise, overcome and adapt!** The choice is yours. And after a good bit of work, you'll be able to plan your **custom-tailored** life, and enjoy the hell out of it.

So then, just "Why" you have a post traumatic stress disorder doesn't really matter. That you "do" have it, does.

Deal with it in a constructive way. Allow others to help you, and there are a lot who will, and not just the $200.00 an hour club.

Pick your counselors and friends carefully, remembering that "like experience" counts a bunch. And just in case you're wondering, I didn't "make up" that list you just read while I was mining for nose gold. I lived and felt every single one of them. And like I keep repeating for the sake of my Marine Pups, "If I could do it, so can YOU!"

Life can be anything you desire, and what you desire can make your life worth living............. Semper Fi!

151

Traveling in a convoy along Highway One, which was actually just a half-assed dirt road, and not really a highway at all, we passed the usual small villages, with "mommasan" and the kids running out and yelling, "Maline, maline, yu buy, yu buy!"

They'd hold up everything from bottles of "fake" Jack Daniels, to bricks of "Mary Jane" (marijuana) and half-dollar sized balls of hash. Hell, it was just like the farmer's market back Stateside in the 60's. I must say that parts of Vietnam were as beautiful as any place featured in travel magazines. It was just a shitty place to fight a war.

We had just come off a major operation, and were filthy, hungry, tired, pissed off and generally in poor spirits. Besides, bouncin' around in the back of an open truck bed, covered with dust for hours, didn't help our attitude much either. And of course we were all "locked and loaded," just in case old momma-san decided to toss a little free treat our way. That is, a home-made satchel charge, compliments of her husband, Charlie.

For some reason and I don't know why, or could have cared less at the time, we pulled into a civilian gravel yard. It looked like any typical materials handling business you'd see in this country. But it wasn't in this country, it was in the land of the Little People.

Anyway, the convoy stopped and after a few minutes, this dumb-ass civilian walks up to our truck, walks around to the tailgate, and for no reason I could figure, says, "Man, all you guys are a bunch of stupid assholes!" Way wrong thing to say to a bunch of pissed off combat-hardened Marines!

In one single motion, our safeties clicked off and all of the loaded M-14s were pointing at this shit bird! Our compassionate and sympathetic reply was, "Fuck you, cock sucker!" "Let's do this lump of shit!" and one Marine yells out, "I've got his ears!" (you know, as in make a nice ear-necklace for mom back home).

Well, this son-of-a-bitch turned as white as a ghost! And as he was takin' a dump in his nice, clean khaki shorts, with his arms stretched straight up in the air, he yells back, "Don't shoot! Don't shoot! I didn't mean it! Don't you guys know who owns this gravel yard?"

Since I was riding closest to the tailgate and had the "cleanest" shot at him, I said "No asshole, who?" He nervously replied, "I–t, it'--s LBJ!" (That was our wonderful President at the time). Another Marine called out, "Who gives a fuck, let's cut off his dick anyway!"

Well, I could see that this civvie had been taught a quick lesson in Marine Corps diplomacy, and being the highest rank in the truck (corporal E-4), I called off the "junk yard dogs." As we all clicked our safeties back on, and the "necklace-maker" twirled his K-Bar with a smile on his face, the "I-just-shit-myself" civilian went on to explain more about how we were all being "fucked for the bucks" by our "My Fellow Americans" leader. When our new civilian buddy (?) was on about his tenth apology, the trucks started their engines, and we pulled away, watching the gravel yard disappear in the dust. We were on our way back to base, with a little more "intel" than any of us wanted to know.

Besides the usual, well thought out and intellectual Marine comments, like "Fuck me," and "No fuckin' shit," we all just kinda stared at each other, pretty much in silence all the way back to our vacation resort.

My best guess is, that civilian was so afraid of dying on the spot, that he did in fact tell us the truth. But you be the judge of that. I've never cared for most cake-eatin' politicians anyway, so I tend to believe that there was at least "some" amount of truth in that civilian's story. Don't really know for sure. A while back I heard a good definition for politics. Poly means "many", and ticks are "blood suckers." Seems to fit a lot of them in my simple way of thinkin.

"So what's the point of all this?" you ask. It's just that in that moment, in that truck, in the middle of a war, I had a "wake up call." If it was completely true or not, doesn't matter. And I think that many of you young Warriors may have had that same uneasy feeling that I had years ago. It might make you feel a little helpless, a bit uncertain, and maybe even pissed off.

You volunteered to fight to defend this country, just like I did. Your brothers, and now sisters, either have been, are, or could be body-bagged just like mine were. And deep down, you know that in at least some small way, that civilian in the gravel yard was right. You may be "fucked for the bucks."

So how in the hell can you feel better about any of this? How can you get past feeling that you were "Right On" in doing the honorable thing, and yet were betrayed while doing it? Well, my friends and fellow Warriors, your asshole may be a little sore, but it probably wasn't the "Green Weenie" (military) that did the deed on this one, it usually isn't. It's just a few greedy bastards in powerful positions after a whole bunch of money. But what you decide on this issue is up to you.

It doesn't make me feel "warm and tingly" to know that where I once stood guard duty (on our rest break) at China Beach in Vietnam, there are now (from what I hear) American hotels and restaurants. It was the same in Korea, and I'd imagine when the dust settles in Afghanistan and Iraq, it'll be about the same. Who knows, maybe they won't let the infidels sell fried chicken, or "Happy Meals." In the long run, it seems that this issue is something that all of us Vets just have to deal with, besides everything else.

For you Young Veterans, there are a few things that you can take away from your experiences in these new wars. Just like us Old Timers did back in Korea and Vietnam. Consider this: You're fighting for your fellow Warriors, because you've chosen to be a Warrior. Just that simple. And you "Know" and "Feel" things now, you couldn't possibly have known or felt unless you were in a war. As an example, I fought for my fellow Marines, the Marine Corps, and the principles of Honor that I believed in, even if others "didn't" believe in them. My reasons, my justifications, my disappointments, became a very personal matter, only to be understood by other Warriors who shared in the same experiences, the same theaters of battle.

I have always loved this country, just not some of the people running it. And in all fairness, there still are some real good politicians around, if they just don't get **sniped** before they have a chance to do something useful for our Nation.

So each of you is gonna' have to decide what makes sense to you, what makes you feel good about the "Whys?" And rest assured, you will figure it out. You Youngins are a lot smarter than this Old Marine was, and it won't take you so long, if you haven't already done it. But remember, if along in the figurin', you start to hatin', remember that "hate only makes you miserable." So don't hate anyone, **"just feel better when they're not around."**

Alright then, besides the "wake up call" and the "whys?", while you're sittin' around on your ass eatin' MREs (Meals Ready to Excrete), let's consider some of the other "Gifts" you've received from war.

First and foremost, you have truly learned the **"Meaning of Honor."** That will stay with you for the rest of your life. Those who do not live by a Code of Truth and Honor are dishonorable. That's just the way I see it, black and white. And you may have to exercise a little patience, because sometimes it takes awhile to express this in your life, according to the high standards it demands from us all. So don't be too quick to judge, because everyone may not be as far along as you are, but still on the way. And especially, don't judge yourself. Everyone makes mistakes and has a bad day. If you can, just don't make the same mistake twice.

You now know the meaning of **"True Friendship."** That is to say, a bond of loyalty and trust that goes beyond words. And that will be your standard for every relationship you ever have.

Your **"strength of character"** and willingness to sacrifice for others has been tested, and proven you worthy to be called a Warrior, in the most intense and extreme conditions the battlefield has to offer. This has taught you your limits and abilities in any situation you will ever confront.

And my friends, you have come to know the **"Nobility of the Human Spirit."** It has been said that, "when conditions are at their very worst, human beings are at their very best." And you have seen firsthand, the very best and the very worst that humanity has to offer. This understanding will serve you as a guide, that you do not judge others for their weakness, and help those without your level of strength.

You have painfully come to know the **"Frailty of Life,"** how delicate is the line between the living and the dead. This knowing makes all life precious, to be taken only as a last resort, never without just cause, and protected at all cost.

You have also learned the value of **"Living Each Moment"** of every day, **"Taking Nothing for Granted"**, and cherishing each and every experience of Joy that comes your way.

You have learned to believe that **"And this too Shall Pass"**, when at times you feel you are pressed beyond your limits, and conditions seem physically and mentally unbearable. But you also know that any situation can always get worse, therefore you are content that it's not as bad as it could be.

With all of your abilities you prepare for battle, and yet pray to God that battle never comes. And through this, you learn to **"Be Forever Vigilant"**, and yet forever grateful for the quiet moment, for the peace that comes unexpectedly, passes too quickly, yet does not go unnoticed.

These, my Brothers and Sisters, are the Gifts of War. Gifts that have indeed come at a very high price. And yet, would you now really choose to give them up, to go back to a time before you held this "Knowing?" Would you now truly choose to become that person "you were", or live the life you once led? I don't. And once you get through a bit of work, I doubt that you will either.

I'm gonna let you in on a little secret. Don't know if you caught it earlier in your reading. You ready? Here it is:

Once you Know, you can never not know again.

Think about it.

So then, cherish your gifts of War and your gifts of Life, plan your new future, and get on with living it. The choice is "Yours". Choose "Wisely."

You can take off your body armor now, lay your weapon down (within reach), and open up a cool one. You've earned it. And **"You've made it through!"** The last section of this book is in friendly territory.

So Enjoy!

5-5 A Warrior's Prayer

I thought I'd include this prayer. It seems to fit, and it works for me. Maybe you will at least find it interesting. As usual, I can't say where it came from, but it does make a point.

Dear Lord, as I move out upon the battlefield this day, grant me the strength to do what all Warriors have always done.

I know you do not judge me in war, nor do you judge me in peace.

You only Love me as your own.

And with that held fast within my heart, I truly walk through the Valley of Death, fearing only that I do not become the evil within it.

Bless my loved ones at home, Lord, that they may never see through my eyes, nor feel through my heart, the loss, the memories that war has given me.

And God, if it is your Will that I return home from battle, may those I Love, forgive and accept me for who I have now become.

Thank you Lord, if I live out this day, and thank you God if I die this day.

For I have learned that each day lived in Faith, Truth and Honor is a day well lived.

It is not for you my Lord, but the Warriors' Code that I fight, that I kill, or shall be killed.

And I know full well, that none of Your Children are called enemy, regardless of race, religion, creed or color.

We are all Warriors, and do what Warriors must in war.

I Love you my God, with all my heart, and I serve you, God, with all of my strength and honor.

Thank you Lord, Amen.

Section Five Summary

5-1 A Tribute to Nurses and Doctors; Heroes All

- Non-combatant medical personnel have as much if not more traumatic stress than those in combat.

- If you are in this group of Heroes, you'll need to get into the PTSD program as soon as possible.

- If you can't find a group session with "like experience" Veterans, maybe you can find a "Friend" from your unit, or range of experiences.

- You will need to "process" all the same emotions that we've talked about in this book.

- Don't deny yourself a good life, by denying you have a problem that needs addressing.

- Help is available now, and professionals have had a long time to work with Veterans like you.

- It's perfectly "normal" to feel what you do, but these problems "don't" just go away. They'll be with you for the rest of your life. Better to deal with them now.

5-2 Post Traumatic Stress for Civilians

- Civilians have exactly the same symptoms that military personnel have.

- You will need to follow the exact same steps as combat Veterans.

- Your traumatic experience or experiences are just as intense for you as any veteran. We all have equally heavy back-packs.

- Do not deny you have a problem, it can be

destructive and fatal if you try to ignore it.

- If you seek professional help, try to find a counselor with similar experiences. No one can understand how you feel, unless they feel the same way.

- It's perfectly natural and normal to react to a traumatic experience and have that experience change your life.

- You will never be the same as you were before the traumatic experience, so deal with it, and get onto planning your life accordingly. It "will" be different.

- Remember, you don't give in to it, and you don't get rid of it. You just allow it to be a part of your life that doesn't ruin the rest of your life.

5-3 Why Do I Have a Post Traumatic Stress Disorder?

- Doesn't matter why or how the PTSD arrow is stickin' in your ass, you've got to deal with it.

- Go down the list of possibilities of what "may" be troubling you. And be honest.

- You can keep the truth a secret for a time, but find someone with your same experiences and eventually, talk about it.

- When you've come to terms with the problems you have, seek out the Veteran's Outreach Center in your area, and run it by a professional.

- You are under "NO" obligation to simply talk things out a bit. So what do you have to lose?

- Remember, you are not "Alone", and others have been right where you are right now.

5-4 The Gift of War

- If you've had your "wake up call", don't sweat it, you're not alone.

- You'll have to decide the "whys?" of the war.

- You'll have to eventually deal with "reconstruction" after the war, and why you were there in the first place.

- You were fighting or are fighting for your fellow Warriors and Honor.

- There still are a few good politicians, don't forget to vote.

- You've learned the **"Meaning of Honor"**.

- You've learned what **"True Friendship"** is all about.

- You have been "Proven and Tested as a Warrior".

- You have seen the very best and the very worst that Humanity has to offer.

- You live each moment, and one day at a time.

- You take nothing for granted, and enjoy the little things in life.

- You have learned to be vigilant at all times.

- You respect and cherish all life.

- And you now have the "Knowing". You can never not know again.

Section Six: Use It or Lose It; It's All Up To You!

1. Where Do I Go From Here?

2. Inspiration is on the Way!

6-1 Where do I go from Here?

Let's say that you've made it this far in the book, and just maybe, you've decided that you might be a can or two short of a six-pack (like yours truly). It really doesn't matter if you're in the military, out of the military, never been in the military, or don't even like the military. Makes no difference. Fact is, you ain't linin' up **center bubble** on the big level of life.

You may have thought that you were "just the greatest person," a little twitchy maybe, and couldn't figure out why everyone went silent when you stopped over for a quick visit. But it sure didn't have anything to do with you? Then suddenly it dawned on your dim, cluttered brain, that if it weren't for your dog and cat, you'd be alone most of the time. It really got bad when you started reading all the labels at the market, because they were all so interesting, and picking up enough movies to last a week. Just because you'd get all dressed up, then jog in place for an hour, meant nothing at all.

Finally you admitted, it may be OK if you went for a "quick" visit to the VA Counselor, or a Civilian Shrink. Nothin' wrong with you of course! You only want to go to talk about a "Friend" of yours, who might have a problem. You know, just to help him (or her) out a bit. Gosh, what a wonderful giving person you are.

Alright, let's cut the bullshit and move along here. If you bought or borrowed this book, chances are, it's not for your invisible playmate, or your blow-up doll, it's for you. So then, if this book "Is For You," and you line up with any of the symptoms in Section Five "Why Do I Have PTSD?" then consider the following few steps as a rough guide line. Remember, that everyone is a little different, and you'll need to custom tailor their own program. This will at least get you started down the right trail.

1. You toughen up, get over your denial, and admit to "yourself," you've got a problem. That's the first "big" step. And it's the only way you can start the healing process. The sooner you start, the sooner you'll be able to see some progress. The longer you wait, the harder it will eventually

163

be. You can't escape the fact, that it's gonna' affect your life one way or another." So don't let it get the jump on you from out of the shadows.

2. You hook up with a counselor (psychologist, psychiatrist) that has had "similar experiences." Maybe you can get into a group session with Warriors just like you. I always liked the group meetings, because it made me feel like I wasn't the only one with something to talk about. I'd even hang around for hours talking to other Vets before and after the meeting.

But be advised, once you do start the process of healing, it ain't an over-nighter. You know, "it's-over-in-a-few weeks" kinda thing. It could take many months, or even years to shake out the Boogie-Man (or Woman), whip his ass and put him in a safe footlocker with a nice big lock on it. You let the sucker out when you want a little "kickin' ass" exercise.

3. Now, in the process of "hookin and jabbin" with your twisted, deep-fried brain, you can start to plan out your new life. Remember, that from the time of your traumatic event (or events) you have "changed into another person." It's like the "Traumatic Event Bird" swooped down on you and laid a shit-covered egg in your head. (Egg head?) That egg is "There" and you ain't gettin' it out before it "Hatches!"

Now, what comes out of the egg is up to you. It can be a "Brand New" beautiful, thoughtful and somewhat twitchy human being, who is an asset to Society, or it can be a troubled, paranoid, hateful person who isn't much better than what was left on the outside of the egg. You know, a shit-head.

Your life can be bright and promising, or covered with a brown substance that nobody wants to be around. You decide. But I can tell you, the "Brown Out" ain't no way to go. I've been there in Fly Paradise, and I like the "Brave New World" a whole lot better. So will YOU! Your new life- plans will probably change a bit as you move along in the process, and get away from the egg-shell. And we'll talk about that in a bit.

4. As you feel better about "Yourself", you'll feel better

about the possibilities of a really good life ahead. But don't quit the sessions at the first sign of progress and improvement. Just hold off on that move to Nome, Alaska for a bit, or that pineapple field in Hawaii. When it's time to make it on your own, you'll know it, so will your Counselor. When I moved around a lot, I always made sure there was a VA Center close by, just in case I needed a little support base. That is, a friendly Landing Zone, to relax and regroup.

How do I plan out my "New Life?" you ask? Well first of all, you'll have to figure out what makes you feel good about living. And no matter what anyone says, this decision **"Is up to you and you alone"**. I'll give you an example.

I was living in beautiful San Diego, married to my first wife, and it happened to be garbage day. That was usually Wednesdays for everyone on our particular block. You know the old saying, "Once a Marine, always a Marine," and even though I was out of the Corps, and my brain felt like burnt, deep-fried chicken, I was still ready and able to lift heavy things.

Back in the 70's, garbage cans were like public restrooms, on the side of each one was printed (in invisible ink) "Men Only." Anyway, in doing my duty as a good husband that morning, and hoping for a "cookie" on my return, I grabbed the garbage can (no sweat for a Marine) checked for snipers, and went out to meet the garbage truck.

Sure as shit, it was Wednesday in California and the truck was on time! The driver backs up close to the row of full garbage cans, gets out of the truck and is "humming a tune" as he's emptying the trash. He was about my height (6' 1") or so, but didn't seem like he really had the build to be wrestling heavy cans all day. And his "horn-rimmed" glasses just didn't seem to make sense to me either.

When he got down to where I was standing, my curiosity got the best of me. So I asked him how long he'd been a garbage man. By the way, that was before they became Sanitary Engineers. So he perks right up and says, "Oh, about two weeks!" Then without any prompting, he tells me his story.

"I was an architect back in Boston," he said. "My parents wanted me to be an architect and paid for all the college. My wife wanted me to be an architect and even picked out the house she wanted us to live in. Hell, everyone had my whole life planned out for me." Then he said, "The only problem was" and he looked me straight in the eyes, "I didn't like my life at all. I really didn't even want to go to college. Kind of liked the idea a being a mechanic of some sort. So, I left Boston, my parents, and my wife in "her" house, and moved to San Diego." Then he said, " I would rather be a Happy Garbage Man in California, than a miserable architect in Boston. And besides" he added, "the money is good, the weather is great, and I get to surf!"

Pretty interesting isn't it? OK, I'm not sayin' you have to be a "Surfing Garbage Man" in California to be happy with life. I'm only saying that it would certainly be nice to be happy.

So let's have a little review, and I'll make a few suggestions. Make that list up of all the things that "You" think would make you feel better about life, maybe even happy. Then like I said before, put in on your refrigerator or a good spot that you see all the time (Bathroom? Foot locker? Closet where you hide the Jack Daniels?).

This is a "No Holds Barred" exercise! And I mean the crazier the better. Maybe you'll want to move to Australia and dive the Barrier Reef, go back to school to be a Forest Ranger, or hike the Himalayas. You might decide you want a new motorcycle so you can take off and tour America. Or you might want to work with kids and animals, join the Peace Corps, work with Habitat for Humanity in New Orleans. Hell, you may wanta' shave your head bald, or grow a beard (men only, please), join a biker gang (Oops! I mean club), or go out and hug a bunch of trees. Who Cares! The only "condition" with this exercise is that it has to be what "YOU" want, and not what someone else wants for you. Just remember the "Surfing Garbage Man."

The point is, that you're gonna' have to pick something new, because you are **not who you were, and never will be**. So why not enjoy the new you while enjoying the hell out of something interesting and exciting? And there really isn't any rush, but why not start now? Take out a piece of paper and have at it. I guarantee you that as your self-esteem grows, your goals will get bigger and more exciting as well.

You'll have lists and pictures of exotic destinations plastered all over your home. Think about it. And if you have a family even better! Make it a family project and get the kids excited about it. It can truly be fun to be planning all this exciting stuff either alone or with someone you love.

That is, as long as you don't shit in your mess gear. You know, make life un-tasty. Don't be your own worst enemy, and cause everything you do to go wrong because you hate yourself. The quitters and whiners always say, "Oh, if I only had a chance. Everyone's against me," and "I only wish I'd get a break." Well, my fine twisted friends, I "am" giving you a chance, nobody's against you, and this "IS" your big break! So don't blow it.

If need be, put your macho pride in your back pocket, or better yet shit-can it, get started on some counseling, and get on with a new, productive and exciting life. Every day, every month or year that goes by, you'll never get again. Don't piss it away like I did.

Feeling good about yourself, makes you feel good about life. And when life feels good and you're in the "Flow", your every desire, your every dream can become the moment you're living within. You just have to work at it a bit. And you "will!"

6-2 Inspiration is on the Way!

As you are planning your new life, you will definitely be inspired along the way. And it's very likely that this moment of direction will come when you least suspect it, and often quite by surprise. It doesn't matter where you are, who you're talking to, or even if you're watchin' the lobotomy tube (TV: severs all conscious intelligence).

It could be a "one liner" from the mailman or checkout clerk, and Bam! You're off to Costa Rica, planning a trip to Disney Land, or starting a new career. And you'll have to follow your leads carefully, to be a good tracker, to stay on the right trail. You know, like a rat following cheese! His beady little brain is "on" the scent, and he's not givin' up until the trap nails his ass. But do not be concerned, because the only trap you'll need to watch out for, is sliding back into thinking you're "just like you use to be." You'll know when that happens, because your eyes'll turn red, you'll be craving cheese, and be shittin' pellets.

I'll never forget my first moment of inspiration. The year was 1965, the location M.C.R.D. (Boot Camp) in San Diego, California. Yeah, I'm a Hollywood Marine. Don't mind at all, cause I never cared for the thought of bein' a Gator Banger at Paris Island. (another Marine boot camp)

Well anyway, we were all standing in formation one fine morning, getting our asses chewed out for what, I don't recall. Doesn't really matter, because that was the usual "wake up, you sleepy head, rub your ass, get out of bed" procedure. And our D.I. (Means: Drill Instructor, or Divine Intelligence) was in rare form. He was an unusually large Marine, built like Arnold Schwarzenegger and about the meanest son-of-a-bitch I'd ever met.

Standing at attention, with eyes fixed straight ahead and bodies rigid, we were being informed of our **low life** status, as the "Predator" paced up and down in front of us, speaking in wise and wonderful ways.

By mistake, I copped a quick glance in his direction. But the keen eyes of this neckless Marine caught me red handed.

"Oh Shit!" I thought, as the D.I. swooped in on me like a

hawk on a rat!

He started yelling my name, and how he was gonna "beat me like a red headed step child!", as he closed in for the kill, ending up not more than an inch from my face.

"Brandi!" he yelled. "Sir, Yes Sir!" I replied. "You scum sucking maggot!" "Sir, Yes Sir!" "You eye-ballin me Boy?" His hat (cover) pressing against my face. "Sir, NO Sir!" I yelled back. "Lookin' leads to likin', and likin' leads to fuckin'. You wanta' fuck me boy?" "Sir, NO Sir!" I yelled while waiting for the usual punch to the gut! (D.I.s could hit recruits in those days)

"Where you from you shit eatin' maggot?" he affectionately asked, while pulling me up off my heals with both of his paddle-like hands (I was still standing). I quickly yelled back, " Sir, California Sir!"

He let go and took a step back, with a faint smile of satisfaction, while I desperately tried to regain my balance, not stepping out of formation. With a smug tone of confidence, he said, "Only steers and queers come out a California you shit bird, and I don't see any horns on your bald-ass-scrotum head!" "You MUST be a queer-bait Californicator!" "Sir, NO Sir!" There was no escape. I was dead meat!
Even more pleased with himself over scarin' the piss out of me, he peered around for another prey. Then he got right back up in my face! And said, "Brandi! You worthless fucking maggot!" "Sir YES Sir!"

"Whale shit sits at the bottom of the sea, and you're fucking lower than whale sit!" "Sir, YES Sir!"

And there it was! His magnificence had spoken. My newly forming green mind was inspired to work in the Ocean! A few years later, I was the Diver/Collector for Sea World, in San Diego, and ran the Marine Aquarium. So you see! Your life can be motivated to change direction from any possible input!

You remember me talkin' about the Buddha? Well what I really liked about old Gautama, was that he said things in a way that even a Marine like me could understand. You know, small words and real simple. He said that **"All we are is the result of what we have thought."** Now that made sense to me, just like the arrow stickin' in my ass.

So if you believe that "what" you think, goes on to control your actions (what you do) then you'd better be careful about what you're thinkin' all the time. For example, if you're not getting some good help from counselors or other Vets, and you're stuck in that PTSD world of hurt, then you're most likely thinking thoughts that aren't doin' you a bit of good. Any thought you think while you're irritated, depressed, grieving, or generally in a pour state of mind, is "not" gonna' make for a bright and cheery future.

The sooner you **"change your thoughts"** the sooner you'll start feeling better about yourself and your life. In the Eastern Teachings, they talk about Karma. You know, "What goes around, comes around." Now, it's not always "bad" Karma. There is "good" Karma too.

Basically it all boils down to this: If you do good things, good things come back in your direction. If you're a shit head, then guess what drops out of the sky, compliments of that large winged lizard that Murphy enjoys ridin' around on?

Personally, I like the idea of being responsible for my own thinking and my own actions. I don't want anybody taking charge on my duty watch. And I figure that anyone not afraid of a "salt shaker" (spineless) probably feels about the same.

So now, once you start to make some progress in understanding **who** you have now become, you'll be doing different kinds of activities. Your only pastime won't be sharpening your K-Bar and cleaning your M-16 five hours a day, or being camo'd up and standing guard duty in your back yard at 4:00 am.

One alternative possibility would be, that instead of "passing by" a book store, check for snipers, and actually go in. And instead of "just" buying gun magazines or Soldier of Misfortune, try a book. Or at least buy both. I just read a good one that sure can't hurt. It's called the "Secret", by

Rhonda Byrne (Yes Marines, she's a good looker). Anyway, maybe it will help you think of just how to go about getting the things you want while you're workin' on your "new life"

There is only one thing about a book. For those of us less familiar with them, even if they're filled with pretty pictures and clever little quotes, it's still only a book. What I mean is, if it's not just a book you can color in, it might be the kind that can actually help you with some new way of thinking. But, it won't do you a bit of good, unless you "really think" about what it's saying. Then "go out and apply" what it's saying through action.

So what is "Right Action" you ask? Well, I like the KISS theory. That is, **Keep It Simple Stupid.** Right Action simply means doing things that are truthful, helpful and kind. First to yourself, and then to others. It ain't rocket science, is it?

But "walkin' the walk is harder than talkin' the talk," and it may take a bit of time and practice to form new habits. And the **new you** will definitely be forming new habits. So instead of leaping out of the rack (bed) in the morning at 04:00, suiting up (battle ready), then to the delight of your neighbors, singing "One, Two, Three, Four, I love the Marine Corps" as you shuffle through the neighborhood, you might just get up, throw on some Marine sweats, and go for a quiet run while watching the sun come up. And my friends, be easy on yourself. You can still put on your combat boots for awhile. I still don't like low-top tennis shoes, and never wear shorts (Low tops can pull off, and shorts don't protect your legs from the brush in the bush).

So start with little things, and one at a time. And as one "old habit" gets pushed back into the past (who you were) you'll feel better and better with who you've now become. Anyway, that's how I've been doin' it for the past 30+ years. Maybe you'll be smarter about it than I was, maybe not. Doesn't really matter, because it works. You change your thoughts, and your thoughts will change your habits (actions). You like yourself, and you may start to like others. You like " who" you are, and no one's dumb-ass comments will really make much of a difference. Now you can just say "I don't give a shit!"

Look, I'm not sayin' that there won't be times when

someone is still gonna' really piss you off, you know, catch you off guard even if you're "aware of your surroundings." What I am saying is that when you "don't" want to piss away your life, it won't be so tempting to flush the toilet of humanity. No one is worth jail time, and you damn well know, you're gonna feel a whole lot better "when they're not around."

"What is your job?" you ask. Well, that one is easy, and stills leaves you a wide open field of possibilities. Your "Job" is to be an **asset** to Society, not a burden to Society. Just that simple. So start snappin' in on the most outrageous life you can imagine. Keep looking for clues, comments and inspiration to guide you.

Sounds like that little green bug on Walt Disney World. You know, that grasshopper with the hat, or was that Mr. Peanut? Anyway, old Walt was a guy that could really make dreams come true! He didn't listen to that spineless anti-salt-shaker league. He made it happen! And a lot of people did a lot of great things with their lives after working through their traumatic experiences. Here's a couple examples.

Some of you may have heard of the actor, Lee Marvin (Dirty Dozen). Well anyway, he was a Marine private when he won the Navy Cross on Mt. Suribachi. The Medal of Honor is the only higher award given for such bravery, above and beyond the call of duty.

He was with the first wave of Marines that hit the beaches of Iwo Jima, in World War II, and his good friend in later life, was right there with him. Lee's hero and friend was Sergeant Keeshan, who also won the Navy Cross on Mt Suribachi, at the same time and in the same battle as Private Marvin.

These two Heroes, certainly had some major "traumatic experiences", and there's no doubt they both had all the problems we've talked about. When Lee Marvin came back from the war, he wanted to go into entertainment. When Sergeant Keeshan came back, he wanted to work with kids. You know him better by Captain Kangaroo!

"No shit!" you say! Well here's another one. This man was a U.S. Navy Seal, a Super Squid! He was a proven Warrior in Vietnam, with over 25 confirmed kills, and highly skilled in small arms and hand to hand combat. When he came back and got out of the military, he not only became a Presbyterian Minister and a pacifist, he also wanted to work with children, and vowed never to harm another human again.

On his morning children's program, he had to wear long sleeve sweaters, to cover up the tattoos on his forearms and biceps. The kids loved him, and so did America. His name was Mr. Rogers!

These three men went through the exact same healing process as every single Veteran that has ever made it home. They went to war, and came back different people. And like you, they figured out what was going to bring them some peace and happiness, then went about working on it. They didn't quit, and surely improvised, overcame and adapted.

Just imagine the "contrast" between these three heroic people, before and after they went to war. One man became a very successful actor, making great movies, doing what he loved. One man was a Navy Seal, Combat Warrior, trained to kill, and who did exactly that. His brain was fried when he got back, but he dealt with his trauma, chose his "new life" and got on with living it as a Peace Maker. The other man, processed everything we've talked about in this book, also planned his new life, formed new habits, and got on with living his dreams.

Now if these three men aren't damn fine examples for all of us, then I don't know who is. And "Listen Up! You can "do exactly what you choose," just like they did. Same-e-Same. Just that simple.

I wanted some land in the high desert, a small home, some animals, and a very peaceful life. It took awhile, because like I have said, this Old Marine was a slow learner. But guess what? Here I am in New Mexico, with animals, a small home that I built myself, and living a very peaceful life. I got everything I asked for, everything on my "list." You will too!

Every morning I get up early, put on a pot of coffee, then sit outside with my two dogs and one very old cat. While I'm suckin' down a cup of Java and a smoke, we all watch the sun come up together.

I may still be checkin' out the ridge line, always will.

But now, in these quiet, beautiful moments, I'm thanking God, being grateful to be alive, to be a "Warrior", and to live this life "For All of My Brothers and Sisters," who never had this chance.

And to all of you, my friends, my beloved Younger Brothers and Sisters who **do have a chance**, "My Love and Respect to each and every one of you!"

Sincerely,

Sgt. A. Brandi, United States Marine Corps

SEMPER FI!

Glossary of Marine Speech, and Catchy Sayings

A

A. J. Squared Away. Someone who is anal about organization, or just plain organized.

Asshole. Uptight, critical, generally annoying person.

Angel of Death. The Beautiful Round-eyed woman that takes you to the Big Base Camp.

Assume the Position. Drop down and get ready to feel the Goodness. (Pain)

Ass-in-the-grass. Someone in the field. Usually a Grunt.

B

B. Street. Used to be a street in Okinawa filled with bars and fine looking women (escorts)

Big Book of Words. What Marines call the Dictionary

BDUs. Battle Dress Uniform. Military clothing you wear into the bush. Marines called them Utilities, the Army called them Fatigues. Don't know why?

Boot. Someone new to the military, usually in Boot Camp. Or someone just new in the unit.

Boom-Boom. Screwing, in Vietnamese speech.

Bouncing Betty. A kind of land mine, that jumps up out of the ground and blows your balls off.

Bug Fuck. Small, intense, overly active. Also, something driving you crazy.

Brain Fart. Bad out-put from brain-housing-Group to mouth. Bad choice of words.

Brain-Housing-Group. The small cluttered human brain. Green colored substance in the Marines head.

Brain Grenade. Usually a beer, but anything capable of joyfully killing brain cells.

Burn the Shitters. A 55 gallon drum, cut in half, and filled with shit. Burning the shit was done with diesel, over long intellectual conversations.

Bush. Usually means out on patrol in the landscape. Or can mean a bush, vegetation.

C

Cake-Eater. Usually a soft-bodied, self-involved Politician.

Carpet Bombing. B-52 Air strike that makes the landscape look like the surface of the Moon.

Chin up, head down, and one round in the chamber, in case you stick the bayonet. A catchy Marine saying, used by Wise and Knowing Sergeants. Means to be prepared, alert, and ready for the unexpected. Like, "Keep your head down and your powder dry."

Chow Hall. The Gourmet Kitchen of Marines, serving only the finest of foods, and staffed by world renowned chiefs.

Chow. The especially tasty food of Marines. Usually just like Mom used to make, only she didn't shit in it.

Cluster Fuck. Nothing working right, Murphy in control.

Code of Honor. Rifleman's Code. Living Honorably.

Corpsman. A Navy person, medically trained that saves Marines in combat. Said to able to walk on water and change rice-patty water into beer.

Cover. Your hat.

Crabbing. Walking on all fours, as low to the ground as is possible.

C-Rats. C-Rations. 12 delicious selections of canned and boxed foods, complete with a tasty desert and 5 cigarettes.

Crotch. What "only" Marines may reverently call the Marine Corps.

Crotcher. A Marine.

D

Death before Dishonor. A Code of Conduct that Marines live by. Means you die before you turn to chicken-shit and wimp out.

Dee-Dee-Mau. (Misspelled) Vietnamese for get the hell out.

Devil Dogs. Marines. Our mascot is the Bull Dog.

Ditty-Bop. Means to walk casually.

Dinky-Dow. Crazy in Vietnamese, used by Vets from that era.

Dry Firing. Practice firing your weapon without ammo.

E

Eagle Shits. Payday in the Marine Corps. Comes from the Eagle on the Marine Corps Emblem.

Extraction Point. That's your exit point, how you leave location.

F

Flush the Toilet of Humanity. Someone needs to meet Jesus right away.

Frag. A fragmentary hand grenade, with about a 7 second fuse.

Fly Paradise. A brown, shit covered world where some people visit.

Foot Locker. A small green box that you hope no one inspects, and where you hide your contraband. Usually kept at the foot of your rack.

Frosty. Means alert.

FNG. Fucking new guy. Usually someone just "in country".

FUBAR. Fucked Up Beyond All Reason.

Fuck. Noun, pronoun, verb, adverb, adjective, etc. One of the two most useful and often used words in the vast Marine vocabulary.

Fucking A! Marine term for Yes! Right on!

G

Ghillie Suit. Also called a Bush-Tux. Brushed burlap covered clothing, that makes one almost invisible in the bush. Used by snipers. (and crazy Old Marines for fun)

Goat Fuck. Something bad happens.

Green Weenie. Old Marine Corps saying. Usually referred to as being fucked by the Green Weenie.

Ground Pounder. Usually a Grunt. The Infantry.

Grunt. A Marine Rifleman. Use to be M.O.S. 0311.

H

Hard back. A tent having a wooded frame and a wooden floor. 1st class housing.

Hookin and Jabbin. Hand to hand combat with bayonets.

Hot LZ. A landing site that is under enemy fire.

Hump. To walk. Often with a pack and combat gear.

I

In Country. Means to be deployed in a foreign country. Or the foreign country you are in.

Intel. Intelligence(?)

Improvise, Overcome and Adapt! Marine attitude toward any obstacle or situation.

Intestinal Fortitude. Guts

J

Jackin' Your Jaws. Talking.

Jar Head. Referring to the bald Marine head, with a starched cover, resembling a jar or jug.

Jerk Off. A waste of air, someone worthless.

Jug Head. Same-e-Same as Jar Head.

K

Kohuna. Hawaiian Sea God. (Holy man/chief?)

K-Bar. A wonderful Marine Combat Knife, and my friend.

L

Lean, Mean, Fighting Machine. A well trained and conditioned Marine.

Leather Neck. A Marine.

Lifer. Someone who stays in the military for 20+ years.

Limp Dick. Someone usually spineless, worthless, and afraid of salt.

Lock and Load! Put your safety on and cram a magazine of ammo in your rifle.

Lolly Gaging. Sitting around, wasting time.

Low Crawl. Crawling as low to the ground as possible, and very slow.

LZ. Landing Zone. A place where helicopters land.

M

M-14. A wonderful, .308 caliber rifle, that I love as my own child and cherished friend.

Maggot. Usually a Marine in boot camp, before they've been reborn as a Marine. Also a generally worthless person.

Make My Bird. Get out of this place. Fly away.

Mess Gear. Metal, fold-up plates that you don't want to shit in.

Mind Fuck. Common term in the Marine Corps. Means you are confused, or you're being confused by someone or something.

MOS. Military Occupational Skill. What you are best qualified for without screwing up.

MAREs. Meals Ready to Eat. (Excrete). Foil wrapped food, that makes you constipated if you eat it dry.

Murphy. A being that waits for you to make a mistake, to make things worse. Usually flies on the back of a Great Eagle that shits on your head.

N

Napalm. Dropped from Aircraft in air strikes to convert Communists to our way of thinking.

Non-Hacker. Someone who quits, and drops out pukin'.

O

One is none. Two is one. If one of anything can go wrong, it will. Two gives you a better chance. This is especially true in setting explosive charges or depending on military equipment.

Ordinance. Explosives, usually dropped from an aircraft.

P

Pain is Good, Now Feel the Goodness. A favorite saying of Drill Instructors about to make your body feel the Goodness.

PLF. Parachute Landing Fall. A five point landing that's suppose to take up most of the shock of impact when your ass hits the ground.

Podunk. Candy, Twinkie-like crap filled with sugar.

Politics. Poly, meaning many. Ticks, meaning blood suckers.

PTSD. Psychological Training for Self Discipline.

PX. Post Exchange, (Navy). A Store on a military base. Army calls it BX. (Base Exchange)

Q

Qualifies for Extinction. Someone needs to put this person out of his misery. A waste of good oxygen.

R

Rack. Your wonderful Marine Corps bed.

ROKs. Korean Marines from the Republic of South Korea. Wonderful fighters, and greatly appreciated by U.S. Marines in Vietnam.

S

Saddle Up! Means to get off your ass, get your gear on and get ready to deploy.

Same-e-Same. Vietnamese saying meaning "the exact same thing".

Scoop, or Skinny. Information, the latest news.

Scum Bag. Someone fully qualified for extinction.

Shrapnel. Small bits of bombs that travel freely through your body.

Snappin' In. Dry firing your weapon, or paying attention.

Spineless Maggot. Someone worthless, having no back bone and a great fear of salt.

Shit. 2nd most common Marine word, taking the place of most parts of speech.

Shit Bird. Generally one with a poor attitude.

Shit-for-Brains. Someone who cannot think clearly, easily confused.

Shit Tube. A direct drop or short cut to Fly Paradise.

Skivvies. Your under ware.

Spotter Round. Usually a White Phosphorus round that marks the spot for a napalm strike. White Phosphorus is a delightful substance that sticks to you and burns until gone.

Squad Bay. The barracks that Marines call home.

Surrender is Not in Our Creed! Marines do not surrender, and do not quit or give up.

Sweep (or Search) and Destroy. The public relations policy in Vietnam, to make better friends and neighbors.

Screw the Pooch. You've made a big mistake.

T

Thermite Grenade. A hand grenade that produces tremendous head, and can melt through an engine block.

Tracer Round. A bullet that when fired is visible, especially at night. Only problem is, the enemy can also see it and where its being fired from.

Thousand Yard Stare. The spaced out stare of a Combat Warrior, thinking about his her traumatic experiences.

U

Utilities. What Marines call their BDUs. The clothes they wear in the field.

W

When the going gets tough, the tough get going. Applies to all non-quitters.

When conditions are at their very worst, people are at their very best. This is when the tough get going!

Winged Lizard. A bird-like creature.

Y

You don't have to like it, you just have to do it. No quitters, no wimps and no whiners. What we all have to do at times and give it a 100% effort.

Young Pups. Young Marines, Young Devil Dogs.